Otto von Fris

Feeding and Sheltering
European Birds

All you need to know about proper
food and feeding throughout the year

With a special section on help with
nesting in house and garden

Colour photographs by the foremost wildlife
photographers and illustrations by Fritz W. Köhler

Consulting Editor: Matthew M. Vriends, Ph.D.

New York/London/Toronto/Sydney

First English language edition published in 1986 by
Barron's Educational Series, Inc.

© 1983 by Gräfe und Unzer GmbH, Munich,
West Germany

The title of the German book is *Vögel als Wintergäste.*

All inquiries should be addressed to:
Barron's Educational Series, Inc.
250 Wireless Boulevard
Hauppauge, New York 11788

International Standard Book No. 0-8120-2858-9

Library of Congress Catalog Card No. 86-10899

**Library of Congress Cataloging-in-Publication
Data**
Frisch, Otto von.
 Feeding and sheltering european birds.

 Translation of: Vögel als Wintergäste.
 Bibliography: p. 69
 Includes index.
 1. Birds, Attracting of. 2. Birds—Food.
3. Birdhouses. I. Title.
QL676.5.F7513 1986 639.9'78 86-10899
ISBN 0-8120-2858-9

Printed in Hong Kong

7 8 9 490 9 8 7 6 5 4 3

The cover photographs show
Front cover: Coal tit.
Front fly: Woodpecker and great tit feeding in winter.
Back fly: Tits eating suet.
Back cover: Birds at a feeding house.

Photographs
Angermayer/Pfletschinger: page 55 bottom left; Billé:
page 28 centre right, page 55 centre left; Coleman/Helo:
page 55 centre right; Danegger: page 10 bottom, page
27 top; Diedrich: page 9 top right, page 28 top left, top
right; Helo: page 55 top right; Irsch: page 10 top, page
38 centre right; Kerber: page 56 bottom, page 38 centre
left; Krug: page 9 bottom left; Leinonen: page 28
bottom left; Meyers: front cover; Moosrainer: page 28
bottom right; NHPA/Murray: page 20 bottom right;
Quedens; page 55 bottom right; Reinhard: page 27, back
cover; Schrempp: page 38 top right, bottom right;
Schwammberger: page 38 bottom left; Synatzschke:
page 38 top left; Tönges: page 9 top left; Wothe: front
fly, page 28 centre left, back fly.

Translator
Francis Monaghan for Leslie Bernstein Translations,
London.

Professor Dr. Otto von Frisch, son of the Nobel
prize winner Dr. Karl von Frisch ("Frisch on Bees"),
grew up surrounded by every conceivable kind of
animal. His tame jackdaw "Tobby" and other birds
were his childhood companions.

 Otto von Frisch studied biology at Munich University
with one year in the U.S.A. His doctorate, written in
1956, was on "The Breeding Biology and Early
Development of the Curlew". Today he is director of
the Natural History Museum in Braunschweig and
professor at the Technical University of Braunschweig.
In 1973 he received the German Children's Book Prize
for his "1,000 Tricks with Camouflage".

Contents

Foreword

Birds arouse our interest more than any other animal. We like them. Is it because of their colourful plumage, or perhaps their song? Or is it because they can fly unaided—a dream that has always eluded humankind? None of us would want to live in a world without birds. And yet we are destroying more and more of their natural habitats and driving more and more species of birds and other animals into extinction. There were so many around when I was a schoolboy that they went completely unnoticed; today they have disappeared. Others have had to change their way of life completely in order to survive.

Everyone can do something for our birds. The ones we can help most are those that live amongst us—in cities, housing estates, and villages. House martins and swallows are quite content to build their nests in or onto our houses. House sparrows and collared doves build their nests only in the immediate vicinity of their human neighbours. If it were not for the waste we throw away it is very unlikely that they would survive the winter months. Many other birds, however, come to our houses and gardens only in the depth of winter when the food they need cannot be found elsewhere because everything is covered in snow.

When we build feeding tables in our gardens or on our balconies and windowsills we are actually helping our native birds to survive the winter period. But feeding the birds makes sense only if the feeding tables are safe for the birds and if the right kinds of food are offered. You learn how to set about that in the first part of this guide. In the second part I will show you how you can be of help to the birds in the warmer months, too. Farmland consolidation programmes have left us with fewer hedgerows and old trees in which the birds can build their nests. If you are going to build nesting and breeding boxes in your garden or on the walls of your house, then you must be sure that the birds actually have an opportunity to breed and that they can raise their young with the minimum of loss. Starting on page 31 there is a description of how nesting boxes should look and where they should be located so that the birds actually use them.

Although you are probably familiar with most of the birds that come to us in winter and summer, what do you know about how they live? For all readers who would like some information on bird biology there is a section which contains brief descriptions, with details of appearance, habitat, song, breeding habits, and—of particular interest—feeding habits. Feeding stations and nest boxes are, as I have said, undoubtedly of help to our native birds; but they are certainly not enough to guarantee the survival of our threatened species. Truly effective bird protection requires the preservation of their natural habitat and the restoration of a natural landscape. I am certain that this book can play a part in fulfilling these goals. When you have observed birds for long enough and learnt about them, then you too will develop a desire to protect and preserve them.

Otto von Frisch

The Bird's Year

"Free as a bird!" implies that a bird can fly off to wherever it wants; but not even a bird is quite that independent. Birds need both a suitable environment and a suitable breeding place. Climate, along with many other factors, influences how and where they can live. Each year of survival also demands a great deal of moving about; there are birds that migrate, birds that do not, and others that migrate only sometimes and that not very far away. Those that migrate every autumn are called migrant birds; those that stay in the same area all year are called resident or all-year birds; the others are partial migrants. But it is not even as straightforward as that. Some birds do not keep to these rules. The robin and the hedge sparrow are really migrant birds; some of them, however, winter here in the British Isles. They can regularly be spotted on bird tables.

In snowy winters birds are especially dependent on bird tables. This is a model made of birch branches and crates.

Why do they stay? There is no answer to that question. Perhaps, for one reason or another, they are too weak to migrate at the usual time. Perhaps they have already found a winter feeding place which has helped them survive a previous harsh winter. Perhaps they simply "don't feel like" moving on. In any case, they stay. Without feeding places many of them would not survive the cold and snow. The definition of what is and what is not a migratory bird is rather muddled. Nevertheless, I will try to describe it clearly. But first I will need to expand a little on what I have said already.

Migrant Birds

Why do many species of birds leave their summer residence? In the summer months, birds that feed on insects and other small animals can find sufficient food in the British Isles. In winter, food is scarce. The days are shorter and so, then, is the amount of time birds can spend on hunting for food.

Think of a swallow for a moment. It hunts insects on the wing. In the summer the air is full of insects which, in winter, all creep off to their "hideaways". The swallow can find nothing to still its hunger. And so the swallow migrates to the south in autumn. There, because of the warmer climate, flying insects can be found even in winter. In spring the swallow returns to the country where it was born or where it has bred before.

The seed eaters, finches and sparrows, for example, eat seeds of all kinds; these birds also eat insects if they find them. The young in particular are brought up on insects. In autumn there is an abundant supply of seeds and berries which forms the basis for fresh

5

The Bird's Year

plant growth in the following year. Fruits and berries, grains and seed can be found here in winter, too. But if it snows, the food is covered and the birds cannot find it. So, even these seed-eating birds would not find sufficient food if they were all to stay here. This is why many of them migrate.

About two thirds of northern Europe's breeding birds, that is, about 152 species, migrate to the south or southwest in autumn. Of these, 52 winter in the Mediterranean area, 11 in North Africa, 24 in central Africa, 24 in southern Africa, and 3 in south Asia. As yet, nobody knows where 7 of the species go in winter.

Enormous distances are covered during migration. The swift, for example, flies 7,500 miles; the stork, 12,500; and the arctic tern, 22,000 miles a year to escape the hardship of winter and to reach the breeding grounds they have established. The average daily distance covered is between 120 and 500 miles.

At this point I cannot go into the mysteries of bird migration in any great depth. Some of these can be solved by ringing the birds, a task carried out by ornithological institutes and the many volunteers who help them. Ringing pays important dividends. By marking an individual bird we can discover where it goes, how quickly it moves about, whether it always returns to its breeding ground, how long it lives, and much more besides. But the question of how particular species orient themselves during migration has only been partially answered. Some know their routes from experience, the young learning it from the old. Others orient themselves from the position of the sun, and possibly from the earth's magnetic field. However, as I have said, the final mysteries have not yet been

solved. Scientists who work in this field still have much to unravel.

As the food supply increases during spring and the days grow longer, our breeding birds return from their winter quarters—some earlier, some later. Shortly after the thaw or advent of warmer weather the starlings and lapwings return. The orioles and the swifts return much later, almost at the end of spring. And it is these birds which leave again shortly after the breeding period, whilst others stick it out until well into late autumn.

The migrant birds have much to do during the few months they are here. In spring, after their return, they must find a territory, search for a partner and nesting place, build the nest, lay eggs, and hatch them. Then comes the raising of the young, always fraught with dangers. During a "rest" period that is all too short, the birds feed themselves well to gather the strength they need for the journey; and then they are off again. Left behind are the resident birds and the winter visitors

Many birds leave their breeding grounds in autumn. The food supply is not sufficient to allow them to spend the winter here. Swallows gather together to migrate to warmer winter quarters.

from the north. For them our British climate is sufficiently mild to allow them to survive. The bramblings and the waxwings are frequent visitors. They breed in the Far North, but in autumn they migrate here in large numbers to spend the winter. We see them often, grateful visitors wherever food is available.

Partial-Migrants

Then there are the partial-migrants. Actually these are resident birds, but when the weather turns nasty they are off. They do not exactly disappear, but they do most certainly avoid the worst of the winter. As soon as the weather is milder they are back. Many blackbirds, for example, migrate to the south in October. The blackbirds that live in the cities, however, stay. They rely on feeding stations for sufficient food to see them through the winter.

Resident Birds or All-Year Birds

Resident birds or all-year birds are those species that stay in Britain; but even among them there are the most diverse behaviour patterns. Some species stay in the immediate vicinity of their breeding territories after the nesting period is over. The warm south does not tempt these birds at all. They are quite capable of living here throughout the whole year. In winter, many of them are amongst the visitors to the feeding places we provide.

The blackbird is one of the most frequent visitors to bird tables. Its melodic song cannot be mistaken.

Bird Houses and Feeding Places

There are differences of opinion about feeding birds in winter: there are those in favour and those against. I myself am one of those who think feeding birds in winter is a good thing. Birds that winter here, depending on the species, have to rely on the availability of seeds, berries, and fruits or on finding the hiding places of insects and their larvae, pupae, and eggs for food. This is especially true of small birds. A combination of may factors—are here I will mention only singlecrop farming, pesticides, and the drainage of damp areas—has led to a stark reduction in the numbers of seed-bearing plants and of insects in recent years. This can be compensated for in some measure by our feeding the birds.

Feeding Places—the Windowsill, Balcony, and Garden

Birds can be fed anywhere. They are at home on the ground as well as in the air and can get to almost any place they want. They are also resourceful enough to spy out a feeding place, and they possess a good memory, too. Once they have found a feeding place they know to check it out in future. If your house is in open country then the feeding place can be positioned closer or farther away from the house in the open landscape. If your house has a garden then that can be used; even a front yard will do. If your apartment has a balcony then that can be very useful, and if there is no balcony then a windowsill will have to suffice. Birds are not fussy when food is at stake. As a child I even witnessed how tits flew into my sister's room to eat sunflower seeds out of her hand. If my sister was not awake for feeding time in the morning, the tits hopped about on the bed and made noise until she woke up and gave them their rations.

Siting Guidelines
• Access must be made difficult or impossible for predators—especially cats, but also birds of prey.
• The feeding place should be positioned somewhere where it is protected from the weather, certainly not on the bad weather side of the house or apartment. It should also be easily visible to the birds and not close to any dense shelter where a predator could hide. As food will quickly be ruined when

Even in the city a bird house at the window will tempt hungry visitors.

damp, it is necessary to protect against rain and snow. Germs thrive in a damp environment, and spoiled food can be very harmful.

If the food is not hanging free from a branch then the feeding place should have a roof and snow and damp will not detract from the table's attractiveness.

Above left: A young great tit. Above right: pied woodpecker.
Below left: Blue tit. Below right: Robin.

Bird Houses and Feeding Places

Predators and Uninvited Guests

Our feeding place is not in open country. Unlike there, many birds come to a single spot and they will come again and again because we replenish the food. The birds lose their innate shyness if nothing happens to frighten them over a long stretch of time, and a predator has an easier time of it than usual.

A winter feeding place must therefore be laid out in such a way that cats have no opportunities for making a surprise attack on your visitors. So position the feeder in the open, somewhere the birds can easily survey, not up against a dense bush, and high enough so that even a practised jumper cannot reach it. If you want to go one further then it would help, if at all possible, if close by there is a bush, an ivy-covered wall, or some other protective shrubbery for the birds. Some people think that a feeding place should not be accessible to mice, squirrels, sparrows, or jays. Why not? Mice get hungry and so do squirrels and sparrows. They will not let themselves be excluded anyway; they are far too canny for that. I have always been happy to see a wild mouse tuck into leftover seeds that have fallen to the ground or a squirrel taking a few nuts. Such visitors enrich the guest list and the observation prospects.

But if you really do not want any mice or other small mammals at the feeding place, then it is not very difficult to deter them. Simply hang up tit ''dumplings'', feeding bells, small birdhouses, and such like to hang free from a thin nylon thread. If the feeding place is on a stand, then the stand should be clad in tin or some other protective coating. In doing so, however, you should not underestimate the jumping and climbing power of some mice and, of course; particularly of squirrels.

Free-Hanging Feeding Places

Free-hanging feeding places are of particular use to tits. The nuthatch also gets its share this way. You can hang up tit dumplings or feeding bells, which you can also make yourself (see page 20).

But there are also easier ways of presenting the food: for example, you can string together peanuts (in their shells) with other nuts, such as shelled hazelnuts, walnuts, or brazil nuts, and hang them on a thread from a branch like a string of pearls. Pieces of beef suet can also be hung about wherever you like (see colour photos, page 9 and back fly).

Tits are especially fond of this arrangement as they are used to hanging upside down in bushes and trees to look for food, and this type of construction means they have less to fear from their competitors. They can crack open the relatively soft shells of peanuts with their bills but not the hard shells of other nuts. Only woodpeckers and nuthatches are up to these.

You can also make a free-hanging feeding place on your balcony or covered terrace with the help of three branches bound together in the shape of a tree. And by the way, that Christmas tree in your room which you no longer need in the New Year can still be of service as a feeding tree for the birds for quite a while. It does not bother the birds if a few of the needles fall off. Those needles remaining still offer good cover, and if the tree

Above: Siskin at a wicker bird table.
Below: Fieldfare and starling.

11

Bird Houses and Feeding Places

This homemade feeding device with perches is also used by birds which are not good climbers and cannot hang upside-down.

is covered in snow then it will look very attractive indeed.

The Feeding House

Finches, buntings, small soft-food eaters like robins, and hedge sparrows are not such acrobats and need easier access to food. For them, bird tables of various sizes are suitable. The possibilities range from tiny tables to luxury tables with several levels. The smallest can be set up in front of the window, fixed to the wall or sill with plugs and screws. They should have only one entrance, and this should be on the side which is protected from the wind and weather.

There are no limits to how big a bird table can be. They are available in seed shops and pet shops, and there is a large selection to choose from. Feed dispensers are made for grain eaters and have the great advantage that hardly any food is wasted as the birds have to pick out the seeds themselves. None of the food will be picked up by passing birds or ruined with droppings. There is a very luxurious three-storey plastic bird table. The upper and largest storey is cased in glass, and birds enter it by flying in from the bottom. Immediately beneath this is the second storey, which is an easily accessible feeding bowl covered by the larger upper storey. And finally, just above the ground, there is a third feeding place, also covered, which is especially attractive to soft-food eaters, such as robins and hedge sparrows. This kind of feeding place with its different possibilities is always an advantage if it is to be visited by many different kinds of birds. Remember, no matter how unnatural, plastic is an easier material to clean than wood.

Naturally a bird house can also be built by a reasonably skilled hobby handyist.

Feeding Places on the Ground

So far I have only spoken about those kinds of feeding places to which birds fly. But there are species which—summer or winter—look for their food on the ground. It would never enter their heads that there might be something to eat just above them! Fowl are among the species that feed exclusively on the ground; in our case this means pheasants and partridges, but also doves. Of the doves, the most likely to make use of large feeding places is the collared dove, if there is an appropriate landing space. This is something that the ringdove would not do. And pheasants and partridges simply prefer staying on the ground. For them you can set up a so-called den (see illustration): a sloping roof on four props about 2 feet (60 cm)

Bird Houses and Feeding Places

above the ground with the sides draped with pine twigs and other brushwood. On the side which takes the brunt of the wind and rain, the roof may reach down to the ground to avoid blocking access to the food by snow. Pheasants will make most ready use of this type of feeding place if it is positioned in or next to a hedgerow, as they do not like to walk over open areas. For partridges, where there are any left, dens should be positioned by hedgerows or copses in fields. Clearly, these dens will also be visited by finches, buntings, and sparrows.

Watering Places

Most birds drink a good deal unless they can cover their needs from watery fruits or meat. If there is a heavy frost and all natural water sources are frozen over, then they will simply eat snow. Putting a flat dish of warmed water near the feeding place cannot

An ideally arranged feeding house with nearby trees and shrubbery.

do any harm. The danger that the birds might take a bath and then freeze up is often cited, but I have yet to actually experience it happening. Aviary birds quite nonchalantly take

The roof of a pheasant den can slope to the ground. Position in or beside hedgerows.

baths in sub-zero temperatures if they have a mind to. I believe that here, too, it is the birds' natural instinct which is decisive and that they will not do anything which is going to really harm them. Providing water is certainly not a major necessity, as the birds will supply their need for liquid from their food or from the snow.

Homemade Feeding Houses and Feeding Places

Some of you may want to build the feeding place for "your" visitors yourselves. There is little to stand in the way of your own imagination here (see colour photos pages 10 and 27 and back fly). Of course, the same "rules" apply to homemade constructions as to the ready-made ones you can buy. Unplaned pine in planks about 3/4 inch (2 cm) thick is a very suitable building material. The completed structure should be

13

Bird Houses and Feeding Places

For birds that search for food exclusively on the ground, this kind of feeding place is easy to build: remove two sides of a crate, and prop up the corner with a slat.

treated with a non-toxic coating to protect it from the weather. Let it dry well!

Illustrations are the best guide for hobbyists, and the following should certainly give you some useful pointers. The beauty of the construction depends on your skillful handiwork and your patience, or simply on the space available.

When building a feeding house you are your own architect. No building regulations will prevent you from building a romantic wooden house or just a hut. You will build your house according to your own personal taste and skills. With a saw, a hammer, a few nails, and some glue you can build a guest house for birds out of wooden pallets, packing crates, fruit crates, all sizes of wood scraps (including waterproof glued plywood as used in boat building), old drawers, shelving, old chairs and tables—anything.

If you want to build a "nature-house" like the birch feeding house on the back cover, then collect fallen wood or wood from trees which are being felled or pruned. But do not become a tree poacher; you must not saw or pull off branches from trees in forests or parks.

A small elevated feeding house. The sides are made of glass and fixed with glass pegs and cemented inside and out. The birds reach the feeding table through the open underside. The feeding table on the stand is used to attract the birds.

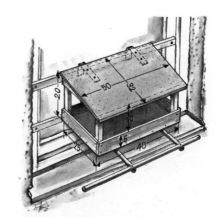

This window-feeding house is easy to fix to the window frame with two crossbars. The open back wall means that the birds can easily be observed through the window.

14

Bird Houses and Feeding Places

Any balcony which is sheltered from the wind and weather is suitable for this balcony feeding house.

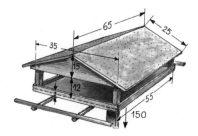

You can count on there being many visitors to a feeding house in a park or garden. Barbed wire around the stand will protect the birds from predators. [The stand should be at least 5 feet (1.5 m) high.]

Proper Food/Proper Feeding

Now it is time to talk about the kinds of food that can be given to our winter visitors. Here, too, people think differently. You will often hear people say that this or that kind of food might be harmful to the birds. I must say that my experience of feeding many types of birds is that animals—animals in general—know instinctively exactly what is and is not good for them.

It is a case of nature looking after its own—at least as a rule. Any bird which is starving to death is probably going to swallow something which is not good for it. But mostly it will only eat things which are good. There are enough kinds of food which will definitely do no harm at all, but if there is the slightest suspicion that food might be bad for the "consumers", then you should not give it to them.

Seed Eaters or Soft-Food Eaters?

Seed-eating birds have strong beaks and can even husk seeds with harder than average shells. Birds that eat soft foods or insects cannot do this. They have to eat the food as it comes. Since you will find both types at your bird table, you ought to make sure both types of food are available to them (see food checklist for our winter visitors, page 19).

The most common seed-eating birds you will come across in winter are sparrows, finches, and titmice. You will also come across nuthatches and woodpeckers, as well as pigeons and fowl. However, this does not mean that these types of birds eat seeds and seeds only. They may very well enjoy other kinds of food but in the main we should feed them on seeds. There are finer and coarser types of seed.

The finer ones are best for finches, titmice, nuthatches, and woodpeckers. This type of seed consists of sunflower seeds, hempseeds, peanuts, and other small seeds. The less fine varieties are best for pigeons, pheasants, and partridges. This type consists of corn, wheat, oats, and all varieties of seeds produced by chaffing.

Let no one come to me and say *they* eat *only* this and *they* eat only *that*. That's not how it is at all. A pheasant is not going to ignore sunflower seeds and a chaffinch is also going to eat corn and wheat. On the one hand, "Needs must when the devil drives," but on the other hand, some birds are gourmets! It is impossible to divide them up so clearly. Nor does it matter much. Then again it is as well to keep an eye on your purse as there is no need to "cast pearls before swine," as the saying goes. A pheasant is well served with corn and a titmouse simply prefers sunflower seeds. I cannot very well set out a precise diet or even a menu for every single species of bird. I can only lay down some guidelines about which types of food are best for certain types of bird, which experience has shown me they like best.

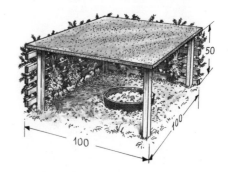

Bird-tables for soft-food eaters should be positioned out of the wind but not up against hedges or buildings.

Proper Food/Proper Feeding

I do not share the view that you should not feed anything which might freeze—fruit, for example, or meat. Some say that birds cannot digest anything that is frozen. But thrushes, for example, will greedily devour apples left hanging on trees even if they are frozen solid. A bird of prey will eat dead hares or rabbits even if the overnight frost has frozen them rock solid.

Meat Eaters

Let us not forget the larger species, such as birds of prey and the crow family. During times of frost and snow they are particularly in need of our help.

They are quite happy to nest on the outskirts of a town or village if there is a possibility of finding food. Buzzards (see colour photo, page 56) and kestrels with their powerful vision will soon find scraps of meat which are put out for them. Offal, such as heart, liver, and the like, is suitable fare for them. You should lay it out in an easily visible spot, cleared of snow, or put it on a tray which has been fixed to a pole. If you intend to watch the birds while they eat, I suggest nailing the meat to the wood so that the bigger birds cannot simply fly off with it. This kind of feeding place is likely to be visited by crows, magpies, and jays, and even woodpeckers are likely to come for their share, too! If the weather should become warmer and the meat turn bad, then it should be replaced with fresh meat immediately (see colour photo, page 56).

The above-mentioned species will all feed on dead meat, but this is not the case with some birds of prey which hunt by day, and especially owls. The small and agile sparrow hawk is, primarily, a hunter of small birds which catches its prey in rapid surprise attacks made either from the air or on the ground. In winter especially, the sparrow hawk hunts on the edges of towns and villages. It very soon notices when birds collect around a feeding place and will not seldom dive in amongst the crowd of sparrows, tits, and buntings to get its share. We should not begrudge it. Sparrow hawks have to survive, too, and their hunting ensures that sick, weak, and old birds have little hope of survival.

Owls, too, have a hard time of it in snowy winters. The mice, their main source of food, do not come to the surface but stay under the snow. Feeding owls is a specialist's task and certainly not to everyone's taste. White or grey laboratory mice should be put into a straw-filled heated tin or plastic bath and placed somewhere quiet during the night. The heating is necessary to prevent the

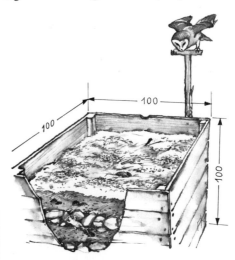

A "mouse box" as a feeder for birds of prey is not to everyone's taste. Expert advice is, therefore, essential.

mice from freezing. Barn owls, long-eared owls, and tawny owls catch the mice in rapid assaults. But it is also possible to attract wild mice, such as wood mice, yellow-necked mice, and field mice, into the right environment. Clear a space in the snow next to a barn or near stables, copses, or on the edge of a forest; spread a thick layer of straw about; and scatter a large portion of grain over it. This will attract the mice and they in turn will attract the owls. But the feeding of nocturnal birds of prey should, wherever possible, be left to experts or carried out only after taking their advice.

Where Do You Buy Bird Food?

You can buy winter food for birds in pet shops or seed shops. There you can buy all manner of seeds, divided into different sorts, so that you can make the mixture of your own choice. But there are also ready-made mixtures available, such as the well-known tit dumplings, tit rings, and tit bells. When buying the food you should check for any parasites among the seeds—principally small beetles—a sure sign that the feed is not fresh. Even in the case of tit rings, a mixture of suet and seeds, it is wise to sniff them to see if they are rancid. This is something the birds do not like at all. You will often find that some tit rings (dumplings) are not very well received—most likely because of the taste.

The soft food suitable for weaker-billed visitors, such as robins, hedge sparrows, thrushes, or starlings, can also be bought in pet shops. Here, too, not all foods are alike. Some varieties, despite being described as "insect feed", contain mostly white bread crumbs and oats. The proportion of dried in-

sects and other protein is very small. Here again you should cast a practised eye over them or consult an expert.

A special treat for tits and other soft-food eaters are mealworms, the larvae of meal beetles. They can be bought in pet shops but they are not exactly cheap; and they should only be given as a "treat" and not in large quantities. However, robins in particular are very receptive to a few mealworms a day and can be made so trusting with these presents that they will feed out of you hand.

Bird Food—Homemade and Collected

You can do a large amount of the planning of your visitors' menu yourself. As birds do not like anything which is rancid, producing your own mixture will be both freshest and cheapest. Use unslated beef or lamb suet which has been melted. This is then mixed with equal quantities of sunflower seeds, hempseeds, oats, or bran until it forms a pulp; put it into small plant pots, coconut halves (see colour photo page 9), or clean plastic containers. The mixture solidifies as it cools. You can hang the containers anywhere you like. Some species of bird will even eat fat and suet on their own.

It is possible to collect and store all manner of things during the summer and autumn which can be used for feeding in winter and will not cost you a penny. Fruit, especially apples, if stored in the right place, can be kept for a short while at least. It will not bother the birds a bit if the apples have a few brown spots. You can also collect walnuts and hazelnuts which, when dried, can be stored for a long time. They will only need to be cracked open with a hammer or nut-

Proper Food/Proper Feeding

Feeding table of our winter visitors

Species	Coarse seeds	Tit rings, feeding bells	Suet	Oat flakes	Dried berries	Insects, mealworms	Chopped apple	Small seeds	Waste grain	Live mice	Meat	Page
Buzzard										×	×	48
Kestrel										×		49
Barn owl										×		49
Tawny owl										×		50
Partridge				×	×			×				50
Pheasant				×	×		×	×				51
Collared T. dove	×			×								51
Gt. spot. woodpecker	×	×	×									52
Skylark				×	×			×				52
Waxwing					×			×				54
Hedge sparrow				×		×		×				54
Robin				×		×		×				58
Blackbird			×	×	×	×	×	×				59
Fieldfare			×	×	×	×	×	×				59
Redwing				×	×	×	×					59
Song thrush			×	×	×	×	×					60
Great tit	×	×	×			×						60
Blue tit	×	×	×			×						61
Crested tit	×	×	×			×						61
Coal tit	×	×	×			×						62
Nuthatch	×	×	×			×						62
Yellowhammer	×			×				×			×	64
Brambling	×			×				×			×	64
Chaffinch	×			×				×			×	64
Greenfinch	×			×				×			×	65
Siskin	×			×				×				65
Bullfinch	×							×				65
Parrot crossbill	×											66
Crossbill	×											66
Hawfinch	×											66
House sparrow	×			×				×				67
Tree sparrow	×			×				×				67
Jay			×	×			×		×			68
Magpie			×						×			69

cracker before feeding them to the birds. Rowanberries—which are not for nothing sometimes known as "birdberries"—are a favourite autumn and winter food, especially for thrushes. They are very common and are easily dried and stored ready for feeding later. Other berries you can use are: elder-berries, privet, hawthorn, and virginia creeper. Dried oats are also a good supplementary foodstuff favoured by soft-food eaters, such as thrushes, robins, and hedge sparrows, as well, of course, as seed eaters. Oats can also be mixed with suet to make tit bells.

Leftover fruit cut into small pieces or boiled, *unsalted* rice and potatoes are also suitable. Bread crumbs, as long as they have been thoroughly dried, especially in the case of white bread, can also be used. However, you should not give the birds kitchen refuse (see below).

What Harms Birds

What you really must not give to birds is anything that has been salted, because it is unnatural. The use of salt and all other seasoning is a human invention. All animals need a certain amount of salt; birds need very little. Their metabolism cannot handle too much salt, and so it is bad for them. Things that we like can be harmful to birds. Everyday kitchen waste, such as the leftovers from luncheon or meat that no longer looks its best, do not belong on the bird table. There are some things you can use, such as oats or unsalted boiled rice, as I mentioned before. But even with bread crumbs and cake crumbs you have to be careful. They should be put out only if you are certain they will not get damp. If you find dead birds at the feeding place then something is wrong. The only thing to do—short of finding the cause, which is almost impossible for the amateur—is to discontinue feeding and clean out the feeding place thoroughly with boiling water and disinfectant, and then the birds are safe to return.

It would be wise to follow these few pointers. That way you will save yourself from disappointment and the birds from harm. You can find pleasure only in healthy visitors.

When Do You Start Feeding?

I have already given my opinion on the question of whether you should feed birds. I am for it. But even if you are for it in principle there are still differences of opinion as to how, when, and how much birds should be fed.

You need to think about when the feeding should begin. Some think you should start feeding in autumn so that the birds get to know of the feeding place early and can find

When making your own food bells you should not forget to include a perching stick. Before filling it with the food mixture you should push a round stick through the hole you have made in the coconut shell (plant pots may also be used). A large hook or nail will keep the stick at the right height.

Proper Food/Proper Feeding

it easily in times of real need. I think this is mistaken. For one thing, in autumn there is still a rich range of food, from berries to seeds and small animals; for another, birds do not need to get to know a feeding place. There are *always* some birds that either know it from previous years or are smart enough to find it in the shortest time imaginable. And other birds will learn of it from them, no matter how few they might be. A very close watch is kept on where food is coming from and who is getting it. Any activity around a table is soon noticed. It is the same thing with vultures: if one vulture finds carrion and circles above it and begins its descent, then others see this from miles away in the air and will rush there straight away. It is enough, then, to start feeding when the first frost or snow falls, when the winter has begun in earnest. At this point, however, you should feed them regularly, not wait until the weather is so bad that the birds are dropping dead from the branches one after the other. It will not take long for that to happen. Even one day without enough food followed by a chilly overnight frost will mean many a bird freezing and starving right on our doorstep. A bird cannot go hungry for long, especially if it is cold.

Feeding Times

We have agreed on which season to start feeding. Now we come to the next question: what time of day should they be fed? This is easy to answer: every morning and evening. In the morning birds have had a long night behind them—up to 15 hours in this part of the world—and they are suitably hungry. In the evening they have to eat enough to get them through the night.

Feed them in the morning before it really gets light. The first of the hungry will already be waiting by then. You should not wait too long into the evening before putting out the food rations or the birds will not have enough time to fully satisfy their hunger. They should be able to start eating 2 hours before dusk. Obviously, they also need to eat something during the day. But there is no sense in filling up the table at midday and leaving it empty in the morning and evening.

The Daily Ration

Again, opinions differ as to the amount of food that should be given. Some say a little but regularly; others prefer "largesse". The golden mean is the best way. There is no danger of birds overeating. Once a bird is satisfied, it will stop eating. The danger in putting out too much food lies elsewhere. In winter, the natural way for birds to find their food is for them to rummage through trees and bushes; to hunt for hibernating insects and their larvae, pupae, and eggs in walls and straw (where there is no snow); or to seek out the seeds, nuts, beechnuts, acorns, and berries still available. The birds should not abandon their natural feeding habits. Obviously, they will be only too glad to do so if their entire needs are supplied at the feeding place. Here they are no different from ourselves. We too become lazy if we are handed everything on a plate.

My advice, then, is: plenty in the morning, a break, a little at midday, another break, plenty again in the evening.

But how much is plenty? Clearly I cannot give exact amounts as it will depend on how many birds you have. If there is a rush, then you will have to provide more than if there

are only half-dozen visitors. You can tell by watching the birds: if they keep on coming back to turn over the husks without finding anything left to eat, if they hunt through every corner, then there was not enough. If there is still plenty of food left in the morning after the birds have stilled their ravenous hunger or in the evening when it gets dark, then there was too much. The otherwise very practical feed dispensers have only one disadvantage in that, if they are kept full the birds can feed from them throughout the whole day. They should only be used in really harsh winters or not kept full. And on that note, a word about the weather in general: it is very rare for the weather conditions to remain absolutely constant throughout the whole of winter, so the amount of food you put out should vary accordingly: more when it is cold and snowy, less when the temperature rises and the snow disappears.

How Long Do You Carry On Feeding?

And when do you stop feeding daily? Clearly that will depend on the prevailing weather conditions. As soon as the frost and snow have abated you can gradually stop feeding. But not from one day to the next! Ease off over 2 or 3 weeks, putting out a smaller amount each day. That will give the birds the time and opportunity to return to their normal feeding habits. If the natural supply is still somewhat sparse, then they will still be able to fill their stomachs with our help.

It does happen in some years that after the thaw, winter sets in again, bringing with it severe cold and snow. Often the first migrant birds, such as starlings and song thrushes,

have already returned from their winter quarters. But even of those birds of which only a small number winter here, such as robins and chaffinches, many will have returned, and in large numbers. In these circumstances we will have to lay the table again. A change in the weather can be especially nasty for early arrivals. Many of them, however, will not accept the food on offer. They are not used to feeding stations and do not know them in the way the birds that winter here regularly do. But one or two of them will follow the lead of others of their species.

When spring finally arrives, the feeding places will empty. The birds have other things on their minds: the mating season is drawing close and territories have to be occupied and defended.

Tits, sparrows, and doves would certainly not ignore a feeding place in summer and would take some refreshment there—but they do not really need to. So do not put any food in summer. It would be a case of carrying coals to Newcastle. Nature's table is richly decked.

Bramblings leave their breeding quarters in the far north to winter in Central Europe. They often come to the feeding places in flocks and search for seeds.

Our Feathered Winter Visitors

Living with Humans—or Without

Of the many birds native to Europe, relatively few are to be seen at feeding places in winter. Of course, this is partly because many species avoid the cold by migrating. Others are tied to particular kinds of food and have no interest in what we offer them. Others again simply avoid proximity to humans. There are those which live with us and those which live without us. This is a rough division we can apply: to animals which "go along with" the changes in circumstances that our influence has brought about and to those which do not. Those which live with us adapt, are fast learners, and show little shyness, even though they may never stop being wary. Those which do not live with us will be driven into contact with people only by hunger or disease. Otherwise they avoid any close contact with the "enemy", people. Their living space is getting smaller and smaller and more than ever it is up to us to protect them (see page 8).

Among those birds which live with us there are some which are astonishingly well adapted; one of the most successful is the house sparrow, which nonetheless remains shy and wary. Others, the tit for example, lose their shyness completely. A flock of tits in England became famous. One or other of them hit upon the fact that there was good-tasting cream hiding underneath the tops of milk bottles delivered to the door each morning. Presumably they were originally attracted by the tops, and pecked at them until a hole appeared. That meant they could get at the cream. Other tits saw this and did the same. Soon no milk bottle was safe. After about 20 years there were already 11 species of bird that had observed and acquired the technique and were using it successfully to open the bottles. The house sparrow was one of them, as were blackbirds, starlings, and chaffinches.

Indeed, birds which live in close proximity to humans show great powers of adapting to new kinds of food and new ways of finding it. I observed a carrion crow for several weeks that had its nest in a tree in a cemetery in the centre of town. It walked over the rooftops and spied under several loose tiles which it obviously knew. It finally became clear to me what it was looking for when it pulled out a sparrow's nest and ate the eggs.

Tits prove how cunning and skilful birds can be when looking for food. They even discovered that there is good-tasting cream swimming about under the milk bottle tops.

That birds do not always make wise choices in their contact with the human world is proven by accounts of blackbirds building their nests under the bonnets of cars or on the steps of a ladder which is still in use! Even crested larks now live amid the turbulent hubbub of big cities, although their original habitat was in wastelands. But they are hard-pressed to find wastelands any more except in cities, in housing estates, railway viaducts, and the like. And so they have made

Our Feathered Winter Visitors

these their own, as have many other species. Most crested larks migrate in winter, but some do overwinter here.

These are just a few examples from many; alongside these birds you will find finches, sparrows, song thrushes, collared doves, and kestrels flying about in town centres. They are not in the slightest perturbed by people or machines. You just have to watch out for them and see or hear them. Most people are unaware of these feathered visitors in our midst and go about business amid the hurly-burly of everyday life not knowing a thing about these birds.

Being Familiar

Some birds are not disturbed by the presence of human beings at feeding places, but there are only a few species which show a certain amount of true familiarity. They have either got to know humans as food bringers or experienced them as entirely harmless. Or else they do not know us at all as they come to us in winter from areas where there are practically no people around. Tits are very familiar, but not all species: mainly we know the great tits and blue tits (see colour photo, page 9), which also spend their summers with us and use the nest boxes as nurseries (see page 32); chaffinches and greenfinches also belong to this category.

Robins are very familiar companions, too (see colour photo, page 9). Most of them migrate in winter, but a few stay behind and overwinter here. As fine-billed insect eaters they are common and constant visitors to feeding places during hard winters, where they pick at the fine seeds and oat flakes. They rarely move away if you approach

them. And if you have mealworms—a delicacy for these birds—it will not be long before they are eating out of your hand.

Blackbirds are also familiar, and they too spend the whole year in close proximity to humans. However, most birds keep a respectful distance and are quick to fly off, and if there is too much disturbance and fuss they are likely to steer clear altogether. If you want to observe them in peace, then do so from behind closed windows and at a feeding place which is a large distance from the house.

The waxwing (see colour photo, page 55) is not at all shy. This is an attractive, pastel-coloured bird about the size of a thrush, with a yellow tail bar and a striking crest on its forehead. It breeds in the far north but winters here with us. As it comes from an area where there are no people, it does not see them as enemies. You can get within a few yards of these birds before they fly off. They have a special fondness for those bushes in gardens and parks which bear berries in the autumn—the favourite winter food of the waxwing. Experts know it by its high-pitched buzzing call. Waxwings fly about extensively in small or large troupes, settling for a while anywhere there is a good supply of food. They will only come to feeding places when there are no more berries to be found and they are dependent on seeds. Here again, they exhibit few traces of shyness.

Rare Visitors

As well as the group of "everyday" birds that visit the feeding places, gardens, or parks in winter—tits, nuthatches, finches, and sparrows—there are also birds which are

Our Feathered Winter Visitors

not to be observed so regularly or in such large numbers. Amongst them are species which are actually migrant birds, a few of which always spend their winter here. The hedge sparrow and the familiar robin are among those I have mentioned several times already. Then there is the fieldfare (see colour photos, pages 10 and 28), which feeds mainly on berries in winter. In late autumn they sometimes migrate in large flocks to the south. Some winter here. They are mainly to be seen in shrubs and bushes which still bear berries. In times of real need, fieldfares will come to feeding places, especially if there are fruits and berries on offer. In earlier times this species of thrush was hunted and captured and was known as the juniper bird, the juniper berry being one of the thrush's favourite foods. Today the bird is a protected species.

Among the finch family there are regular and well-known visitors, such as the greenfinch, the chaffinch, and the bullfinch. They are to be seen throughout the year, even though most chaffinches migrate south in the autumn. In their place come the bramblings from the north (see colour photo, page 55), often in enormous flocks to feed mainly in the beech forests from the beechnuts lying on the ground. It is not rare for them to settle in small troupes at the feeding places, where they search the ground for seeds. Another finch, our largest, which is only occasionally to be seen at feeding places, is the hawfinch (see colour photo, page 55). Its enormous beak, which gives it a nose-heavy appearance, makes it unmistakable. Its bill is so strong that it can crack open the stones of cherries and plums to feed on the edible kernels.

A very interesting member of the finch family is the crossbill (see colour photo, page 55). It gets its name from the tips of its beak, which cross over each other, like those of its more powerful relative, the parrot crossbill. Crossbills feed mainly on seeds from conifers and so spend most of their time in conifer forests, particularly in pine and fir forests. There they perform their acrobatics amongst the branches like parrots, often hanging upside down, winkling out the seeds from pinecones. Crossbills are also known as "gypsy birds", as they move about from place to place, depending on the supply of seeds, and do not have a fixed breeding season. As soon as they find a forest with a plentiful supply of food they begin to build their nests and breed, even in midwinter. As food specialists which still their hunger as described above, they will visit the feeding places only in exceptional circumstances: most likely if it is located in their natural habitat—a conifer forest. In those circumstances the crossbill will also feed on other seeds, especially sunflower seeds.

The siskin, a small yellowish green finch (see colour photo, page 10), behaves in a similar way. In winter it feeds on fine seeds; siskins are very fond of alder seeds. Crowds of these delicate birds can be seen feeding in woodlands and parks. Their frail bills are not suited to opening the coarser and harder types of shells. So, if they do appear at feeding places they will only feed on small seeds for preference, such as hemp and millet seeds, or on scraps of nuts or sunflower seeds.

The yellowhammer was a frequent winter visitor 20 years ago, to be seen on the edges of towns and in villages around chicken coops and stables, where there was always leftover grain. Today this member of the bunting family has become rare in many areas, not only as a breeding bird. It searches for food on the ground, often in the company of tree sparrows and house sparrows.

Although the tree sparrow is not at all a rare species, it is not a very well known one. In summer it mainly lives close to arable land and is rarely seen near human settlements. In winter, however, it does move into villages and onto the outskirts of towns, where it is a common visitor to feeding places.

A Mouse Hunter in Need

Obviously, hunger and cold have their effect. A really harsh winter will turn many a shy bird into a tame visitor which will eat out of your hand. A few years ago there was a blanket of snow which lay undisturbed on the ground for several weeks. The mice were living under it, and the birds that lived on the mice were having a bad time. A kestrel moved into my garden, half-starved to death with no thought left of escape. From a safe distance I threw it a dead mouse, which it grabbed at immediately and devoured on the spot. From that time on it stayed in the garden, grew to expect being fed three times a day, and allowed me to come closer and closer. After 3 weeks it was flying to within 2 yards of me to pick up a mouse: no inhibitions, no fear, no shyness. As soon as the snow thawed it disappeared to hunt for its own food in the fields. In times of need many other species of bird can, like this kestrel, look for and find help from human beings and forget for a while the natural law of hunter and hunted. At such times we can experience, once more, the return of a little

of that lost paradise, a feeling for our fellow creatures which, though not as strong or "clever" as we, still have a right to live on this earth.

The Shy "Whippersnapper"

One might think that house sparrows in particular, living as they do exclusively in close proximity to human beings, would be amongst the most trusting of our winter visitors. But do not be fooled! House sparrows are "cheeky", always around, and can clear a feeding place of food in no time as they always come in swarms, but of all our native birds they are the ones that are most wary and most suspicious and take flight at the slightest disturbance. You will see sparrows only in villages and towns throughout the year; but despite being permanently "surrounded by people" it never lets up on its shyness and wariness. Unlike all too many other animals, it understands how to cope with new situations and to spot all dangers with great speed. A gregarious animal, it always lives in large or small flocks and has so far managed to resist all the persecutions to which humans have subjected it.

Why are attempts being made to curb the "sparrow plague"? The house sparrow has made itself unpopular in several ways. In areas on the edges of towns and villages, in particular, it has caused considerable damage by falling in great swarms on crops shortly before harvesting. In addition, house sparrows are the carriers of the most diverse diseases common to poultry. Their large nests block up ventilators and drains on

Great tit and brambling at the feeding house.

buildings and pollute them with all manner of nest materials and their droppings. They can also cause a not inconsiderable amount of harm when competing for food with chickens and ducks at their feeding places, by consuming enormous amounts of their food. Finally, they can also occupy the nest holes which have been set up for rarer or even threatened species. In the fight for such holes, house sparrows are usually the victors over tits or flycatchers.

Naturally, house sparrows visit feeding places in winter in large droves and consume a sizeable proportion of the food which is available. It is not possible to drive them away—they, too, experience need on hard winter days. However, they do less well on free-hanging tits bells and similar arrangements so that they can be satisfied with oats or bread crumbs scattered on the floors of feeding houses or on the ground. This leaves the "better" things for the tits.

House sparrows are not a protected species, and you can feel free to remove any freshly made nest you discover in a nest box, provided, of course, you are sure what built it.

What You Need to Know About the Protection of Birds

If, today, we save the life of a bird through winter feeding or help it to breed successfully with a nest box then that is certainly a worthy act, It is, alas, still not a great

Winter visitors. Above left: Redwing. Above right: Fieldfare. Centre left: Song thrush. Centre right: Collared dove. Below left: Hedge sparrow. Below right: Nuthatch.

contribution to wildlife preservation. In the case of bird protection, it is no longer just a matter of protecting individual species. Until the beginning of this century the main threat to birds came from their capture, shooting,

The crossed-over tips of the bill give the crossbill its name.

plundering of their eggs, and the persecution of individual species as "competitors" with humans. Now it is the destruction of their natural habitat which threatens this or that species with extinction. Our main efforts must go into preserving these habitats, their biospheres. The Royal Society for the Protection of Birds (The Lodge, Sandy, Bedfordshire) and its junior section, The Young Ornithologists' Club (same address); the British Trust for Ornithology (Beech Grove, Tring, Hertfordshire), the Society for the Promotion of Nature Conservation (The Green, Nettleham, Lincolnshire, and many other organizations involved in the protection of the environment, along with many volunteers, are working around the clock to save or re-establish natural habitats. Drained moorlands are being irrigated, the fight goes on for every hedgerow and copse, and pleas go up for the preservation of old forests and natural mixed forests. But there remains much to be done. We must all ensure that at all times the issues around bird protection, indeed environmental issues as a whole, are brought to the attention of politicians and other responsible persons and made credible through sound argument and then effectively acted upon.

Sparrows are very shy and wary, spot dangers quickly, and take flight at the slightest disturbance.

Help with Nesting in House and Garden

Why Help with Nesting?

The birds' interest in feeding places dwindles in spring. Insects gradually emerge from their hibernation, and fresh greenery is shooting up all over the place. Nature's feeding table is richly decked.

Whatever survives the winter unscathed now has to set about the preservation of the species through reproduction. Birds occupy a territory, find a mate and a place to build their nest, lay eggs, and raise their young. Regardless of whether they breed in holes, cavities, or the open air, it is usually a bad thing for birds if there are buildings nearby.

It is certainly a good thing to set up nest boxes and so help birds with their nesting. Natural nesting places are becoming more and more scarce, particularly in towns and on their outskirts, but even in forests, too. This is not only true of hole-breeders, those species which breed in holes, in trees or rocks, for example, but also of those that build their nests in dense hedges and bushes. Modern forestry has little patience with old and dying trees as they attract harmful insects. But it is precisely these trees which have many holes: woodpeckers, for example, carve out their nurseries in them which are used in later years by other hole-breeding birds.

The hedgerows and bushes that in earlier years could be found everywhere on arable land or on the edges of forests, or even in those forests that are left to replenish themselves naturally, are being cut down and destroyed despite all warnings (see page 29). Numerous other animals and plants are also losing their chances of reproduction and hence survival. There is no question about the need for us to balance out the loss of natural nesting places in some measure by building nest boxes and planting dense shrubbery in our gardens and yards or onto the house and so help the birds with their search for suitable places to nest and have young.

The ins and outs of how and where birds build their nests is so diverse that it is impossible for us to account for all of them here. Many birds even avoid all proximity to human beings; but we can help those birds which exhibit little shyness and remain within our vicinity even during the breeding season, and helping them with nesting is not particularly difficult.

Nesting Habits of Hole-Breeders

In our case it is mainly tits, nuthatches, and collared flycatchers seek out holes to breed in. Holes occur naturally in old trees

The redstart is a hole-breeder. In May, during the breeding season, the male attracts the female to the hole with its lively antics. The female is responsible for building the nest and the incubation. The male helps feed the young.

Help with Nesting in House and Garden

when not every dead branch is sawn off or trunk felled. Even an old garden wall, gnawed by the tooth of time, or an old building will have holes and cavities here and there. Tits are unbelievably skillful at finding nesting places. Even postboxes will be converted into nurseries, or old iron pipes open at the top—even though they do not rarely prove to be death traps for the young when rain gets in and destroys the brood. By and large, however, such nests are a rarity.

Artificial nest holes for hole-breeders can be bought in the most diverse styles from pet shops and seed shops. Highly recommendable are nest holes that are made of wood and concrete.

Nest holes with thin plastic walls should be avoided. They are too hot in summer and too cold in winter, whereas wood and concrete models are well insulated. You may ask, why in winter. Well, many hole-breeders overnight in nest boxes in winter. In harsh winters especially, birds which can spend the night in nest boxes have far greater chances of survival than those that do not.

Nest boxes for hole-breeders made of wood to screw on (left) and wood and concrete (right).

Nest holes made entirely of wood are not bad, but they cannot be cleaned as thoroughly, and they decay and rot in time, which means they have to be replaced more frequently. Gnawing animals, such as squirrels, dormice, or mice, can easily destroy them by widening the entrance and building a home for themselves in them.

As always with birds, when it comes to building nests each species has its own preferences. This is why there are so many types of nest holes on offer. They are available for every size of hole-breeding bird, from tawny owls to blue tits. It is not only the size of the nest hole itself which is important, but also the size of the entrance hole. The table on page 33 will not only be of use when buying a nest hole but also if you want to build one yourself.

You can also buy artificial nests made of wood and concrete or wood for cavity-breeders, too. They do not have an entrance hole but are half-open at the front. They will be used by spotted flycatchers, black redstarts and redstarts, pied wagtails, and sometimes blackbirds, too. They should always be fixed to the wall of a house, a thick tree trunk, or a wall. Nest holes for more rare or "difficult" species of birds, such as owls, kestrels, or dippers, have special requirements. To discover whether it is sensible to position them near houses you should first discuss the matter with your local bird sanctuary or club and get their expert advice. Dippers are only found near clear mountain or sub-alpine lakes. Kestrels and tawny owls, on the other hand, do live in towns if they offer an opportunity for them to breed.

Help with Nesting in House and Garden

Nest Builders—House Martins and Swallows

Our swallows, the swallow and the house martin, have developed their own nest-building technique. They even build their own "holes" of damp clay or earth mixed with all manner of bits of straw or feathers. Both species live in close proximity to humans and build their nurseries in or on buildings, which they use as a substitute for cliff faces. The swallow builds its cup-shaped nests with an opening in the top in stables, barns, and houses in such a way that the nest rests on a support, which can be a beam, a buttress, or just a pipe running along a wall. The house martin, on the other hand, builds its nest on the outside wall of a house under the eaves with only a small opening as an entrance hole.

Both species of swallow are seriously endangered. It is not only the lack of insects which has caused their problems but also a lack of damp building materials in the vicinity of their nesting places. More and more yards, driveways, front gardens, and other spaces around houses are being covered in concrete and kept clear so that the puddles where swallows could collect their clumps of mud are scarcely to be found anymore.

Now, even swallows will use artificial nests, which are also available in shops. They are simple to fix in or onto suitable places. They have an advantage over the nests built by swallows themselves in that the artificial nests last for years whilst their own usually crumble and collapse in winter. In autumn artificial swallow nests need to be cleaned and any foreign nesting material removed.

As house martins breed in colonies you should always provide at least two but preferably several artificial nests placed alongside each other.

Measurement Table for Building Nest Boxes

Species	Thickness of walls	Width of entrance	Entrance wall	Back wall	Side walls	Floor	Ceiling
All native species of tit, nuthatch, pied flycatcher	¾ (20)	1¼–1⅓ (32–34)	4¾ × 9 (120 × 130)	6¼ × 11¼ (160 × 285)	5½ × 9¾ × 11 (140 × 250 × 280)	4¾ × 5 (120 × 130)	7½ × 10 (190 × 250)
Redstart	¾ (20)	1¾–1¼ (45–30)	4¾ × 9 (120 × 130)	6¼ × 11¼ (160 × 285)	5½ × 9¾ × 11 (140 × 250 × 280)	4¾ × 5 (120 × 130)	7½ × 10 (190 × 250)
Wryneck and starling	¾ (20)	1¾–2 (46–50)	5½ × 10¼ (140 × 260)	7 × 12¼ (180 × 310)	6 × 10¾ × 12¼ (150 × 275 × 310)	5½ × 5½ (140 × 140)	8¼ × 9¾ (210 × 250)
Stockdove	1 (25)	3–3½ (80–90)	9¾ × 13⅓ (250 × 340)	11¾ × 15 (300 × 380)	10⅓ × 14 × 15 (263 × 360 × 380)	9¾ × 9¾ (250 × 250)	13⅓ × 14 (340 × 360)
Little Owl	¾ (20)	3½–3¾ (90–95)	6½ × 12¼ (170 × 31)	8¼ × 14¾ (210 × 275)	7 × 12¾ × 14¾ (180 × 325 × 375)	6½ × 6½ (170 × 170)	9½ × 12¼ (240 × 310)
Tawny owl	1 (25)	4¾–5 (120–130)	9¾ × 15¾ (250 × 400)	11¾ × 17⅓ (300 × 440)	11 × 16½ × 17⅓ (280 × 420 × 440)	9¾ × 10½ (250 × 268)	13⅓ × 15 (340 × 380)

Measurements in inches and (millimetres).

Help with Nesting in House and Garden

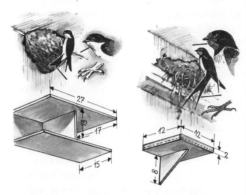

Left: House martins build closed plaster nests with a round entrance hole under jutting roofs and bridges, always on the outside of buildings. To help with nesting, fix a nest niche immediately under the roof.
Right: Swallows always build open plaster nests on the inside of buildings, such as stables, the halls of rural houses, and attics. To help them with nesting, supply nest boards or ready-made nests.

Out third species of swallow, the sand martin, avoids close proximity to people. It builds horizontal breeding tubes on steep sand or mud banks near streams or those produced in the excavation of sand or gravel pits. If the sand martin is not to die out, then such steep banks must be preserved. Often a hundred or more couples will breed together in a favourable spot.

Homemade Nesting Aids

It is not very difficult to build nesting aids for our hole-breeding summer visitors. There are, however, some guidelines you ought to follow so that your efforts will be crowned with success. The table on page 33 will help choose the right size. You should use only healthy and well-seasoned wood; otherwise

your construction will develop cracks within 2 years. Oak, alder, white beech, pine, and fir have shown themselves to be the best kinds of wood to use. Poplar, red beech, and willow should be avoided. The inside surface of the boards need not be finished in any way: you can save yourself the wearisome task of planning, and also your visitors will be glad if you do not coat the inside. The outside, however, should be given a protective coating; this will prolong the life of the nest box. This coating must be non-toxic and completely dry before hanging out the box. A particularly ''upmarket'' product for hole-breeders would be, of course, a nest box carved from a tree trunk. That, though, would be a job for a very patient woodworker.

You can do a quicker job with crates which have been nailed together. In this case you must take care that the boards are joined together without any gaps so even in heavy rain the nursery will be undamaged. It is also very useful to drill two or three holes into the bottom, so that if water does get in it will simply flow out again. There is no need for a perch in front of the entrance hole. Most birds fly straight into their ''front doors''. A perch will only make it easier for uninvited guests to get in.

The ''nest constructors'', the house martin and swallow, both value the nesting help which you give them. The two ''Build-it-Yourself'' brands of nest bases illustrated on this page will readily be made use of. I will also give the bird lover the following to consider: modern building techniques are responsible for the disappearance of these species. Providing suitable nest bases—be they purchased from a shop or homemade—is not the only way to help pre-

Help with Nesting in House and Garden

serve these birds; even having muddy puddles about will be a significant help to them.

To prevent the house walls getting dirtied, something people understandably enough do not like to see, you could put up dropping-shelves, about 8 inches (20 cm) wide underneath the nests. It is advisable to position them at least 20 inches (50 cm) beneath the nest.

Few people are in a position to help the dipper with its nesting as it will only nest near clear lakes and streams. Should these attractive birds live in your vicinity, however, it is possible to make them a nursery (as illustrated) with very little effort which you can position in a high corner of a bridge.

Where to Position Nest Boxes

Nest holes can be positioned anywhere. They can be hung from trees, on house walls, or on the balcony. It is best if they are hanging free from a wire so that your neighbour's cat cannot sit on its roof and put its claws through the entrance hole to fish for the inhabitants. The entrance to all nest boxes should face east, that is, away from the bad weather side. It is astonishing to see

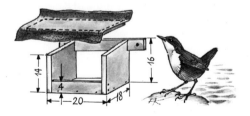

Nest boxes for dippers should be positioned near clear lakes and streams on cliffs, overhanging banks or under bridges.

just how quickly artificial nest boxes do get discovered and made use of. Not always and anywhere, obviously, but as a rule, yes. A new housing estate of bare blocks and little vegetation is not going to attract any birds. There is no cover for them. Small birds need bushes and trees where they can flee in case of danger. They will avoid open and barren terrain whenever possible. But as soon as there is any shrubbery the birds will appear and start looking for places to nest. If a nest hole remains unused year after year then there will be a reason for it. It is either too exposed to wind and weather, there is a lack of cover nearby, or the whole area is unsuitable for the birds. Too many cats in the area, or even just one, can be a reason for a tit not to move in.

Preventing Predators

A bird lover can be caused a great deal of trouble by a neighbour's cat, or even by strays coming from far afield to disturb a group of birds. By law all cat owners are obliged to see that the cat does not cause any damage, especially away from their own property. But in practice there is little to be done about stray cats. As they usually go about their business at night they tend to do so undisturbed. It is rarely possible to drive them off, and if so then it is only for a short time. During the mating season, at least, cat owners should keep their pets in the house at night. This would lead to a sizeable reduction in the number of nocturnal trouble-makers.

Trees with bird nests in them are relatively easy to protect. The cheapest way is to take the longer canes of dog roses or climbing

35

roses and wind them around the trunk to a height of about 1½ yards (1½ m). Not even a cat will want to tangle its paws among the thorns and will steer well clear of such a tree. The canes will keep for quite some time. With a little skill you can also construct more lasting forms of protection from tin or wire to make climbing the tree more difficult for a cat. A 3 foot (1 m) tall tin or plastic cover will also do the trick but will not look very attractive.

It is not only cats that are a danger to breeding birds. Other mammals also hunt in our gardens. The beech martin is not as rare a visitor as you might think. The droll and generally popular squirrels are also nest plunderers. But in the final analysis this is all part of the natural order of things with which human beings have interfered quite enough already. When at all possible, you should intervene only in circumstances in which the predators have the upper hand over the birds, which usually is a result of our influence in the first place.

Should Old Nests Be Removed?

Should old nests—in nest holes or free hanging—be removed in autumn? An oft-put question. You should! Old nests are a refuge for many kinds of vermin. Birds, too, have fleas, lice, and other parasites that collect in old nests, just waiting for a new "guest" to move in, so they can bury themselves under its feathers: Away with the old nests in autumn. The best thing to do with them is to burn them. They are of no use to anyone, except the parasites.

Bear in mind that many of our smaller birds breed twice a year. As soon as the first brood has left the nest hole, the old nest should be removed.

Nesting Places for Birds Which Breed in the Open

Open-space breeders, those species of birds which build their nests in shrubs, on branches, boughs, and trunks, or on the ground, depend just as much on suitable locations as those species which breed in holes. What can we do for them? Which species are they? There is no room here to list them all, but let me mention some of the less common, especially those which do not deliberately avoid human contact, such as thrushes, finches, hedge sparrows, robins and dunnocks, wrens, and warblers.

They build their nests in dense undergrowth, hedgerows, bushes, shrubs, trees, thick vegetation, and dense grass. We need to make sure that all these are available to them. Bushes and hedges do need a year or two until they are dense enough. Meanwhile it is possible to provide artificial nesting places in those areas where, for whatever reason, there is no thick shrubbery for them to breed in. Make a bundle of brushwood, with some furze or pine twigs, and bind it tightly to a tree trunk and you will have made a safe nesting place already. It is also important to watch out for breeding birds and their nests and young when working in the garden in the summer months. It is very easy to uncover a nest when cutting a hedge or pruning bushes and trees. The adult bird will often be disturbed and abandon the nest. Unprotected

A spotted flycatcher feeds its hungry young.

Help with Nesting in House and Garden

A few twigs tied to a trunk are most suitable as nesting aids.

nests are also exposed to danger from cats and from birds of prey. More and more jays and magpies are moving into densely inhabited areas and systematically searching out nests for their eggs and young. This usually happens in the early hours while we are asleep and the gardens are quiet. You may be made aware of the attack by the frantic warning cries of the adult birds, worried for their brood, as they try to distract the predator. They stand little chance against the far larger jays and magpies.

Let us plant hedges and bushes and leave them to grow where they stand! A bare garden, lots of lawn: no bird will settle down to nest.

Foundlings
Above left: Chaffinch. Above right: Blue tit. Centre left: Song thrush. Centre right: House sparrow. Below left: Kestrel. Below right: Long-eared owl.

Help with Nesting in House and Garden

Nest and Nesting Table of Our Breeding Birds

Species	Hole	Cavity	Ground	Tree	Dense shrubbery	In buildings	Onto buildings	Page
Kestrel	×	×				×		49
Tawny owl	×					×		50
Partridge			×					50
Pheasant			×					51
Collared T. dove				×				51
Gt. spot. woodpecker	×							52
Skylark			×					52
House martin							×	53
Swallow						×		53
Pied wagtail		×					×	53
Hedge sparrow					×			54
Spotted flycatcher		×					×	57
Pied flycatcher	×							57
Black redstart		×					×	57
Redstart		×					×	58
Robin			×					58
Blackbird				×	×		×	59
Fieldfare				×				59
Song thrush				×				60
Great tit	×							60
Blue tit	×							61
Crested tit	×							61
Coal tit	×							62
Nuthatch	×							62
Wren					×		×	63
Yellowhammer			×					64
Chaffinch				×				64
Greenfinch				×				65
Siskin				×				65
Bullfinch					×			65
Hawfinch				×	×			66
House sparrow	×	×					×	67
Tree sparrow	×							67
Starling	×							67
Jay				×				68

Raising Foundlings

What You Really Need to Know

Foundlings are quite a problem. In every breeding season there are young whose parents have been killed or who have fallen from the nest or been otherwise injured. Out in the woods you rarely notice them, but you occasionally find them in gardens, outside the house or in town. What do you do then?

To be frank—if you do take one of these young, then in most cases you will probably be breaking the law. Most of our native birds are covered by one law or another: hunting laws, environmental protection laws, protection of species laws, etc. But if a child or a bird lover does find a half-starved abandoned chick, then what? In many cases, of course, the bird will be taken home, looked after, and often successfully restored to health. Every summer I get calls asking me what to feed it, what to do with it when it can fly. Most foster parents go to inordinate trouble and are outraged when I tell them that they are actually doing something that they should not.

There are official bird sanctuaries for abandoned or injured birds. It is just that most members of the public are unaware of their existence and do not know where to find them. They are not exactly thick on the ground. And so people turn to a local institution, maybe a natural history museum, a zoological institute, or an animal protection society. They will advise as best they can.

What I must strongly warn against are attempts at raising birds of prey, owls, or other rare and threatened species. You are obliged to pass such birds over to official organizations responsible for raising and looking after such birds. Nevertheless you may be in a situation in which you do have to look after such a foundling for a few hours or a day before you find out where you may take it (see page 70).

Even granted that you find a chick you cannot assume that it has been abandoned. Usually the parents are in the vicinity but out of sight. The young of smaller birds usually leave the nest late and are normally fed every couple of minutes. You can keep watch from a distance. If no adult bird appears within an hour you are probably right to assume that the bird has been abandoned. If it continuously gives out cries of hunger even in your presence and is cold and clammy to the touch, then you can take it with a clear conscience.

If there is any doubt, keep your hands off! Do consider whether you will be able to reach a place of sanctuary in time. A young bird needs a lot of care. It cannot feed itself; you will have to feed it, and often. Also, successful cases of re-introducing hand-reared birds to the wild are rare. If you still wish to raise the bird, then you must accept the responsibility for its future fate. I will now give you a few pointers on raising young birds.

Lift the foundling gently in both hands and hold very lightly with the thumbs.

Raising Foundlings

What Have I Picked Up?

To raise a young bird properly you need to know its species, or at least its family. This is not an easy as it might seem.

First a word about *nidicolous* birds, those that leave the nest late. Most birds of prey and owls have a white or grey-white down. The upper bill is hook-shaped and pointed, and their claws are more or less curved (see colour photos of kestrel and long-eared owl, page 38). Members of the crow family, with sparse plumage, are difficult for the uninitiated to tell apart. If the feathers have grown, though, and they are black or grey-black, then the bird is probably a crow or a jackdaw. Young magpies are born with the black-and-white plumage of their parents. The mouth of most members of the crow family is of a dark or bluish red colour.

The young of the thrush family's first plumage is a camouflaging ground tone of brown or grey with light or dark spots or streaks.

Young cuckoos or woodpeckers can be recognised by their back toes. These species do not have the usual three front and one back toes but two front and two back (as, by the way, do owls). Young woodpeckers also have the pointed chisel-shaped bill and a thin worm-like tongue.

Young doves have a yellowish down, a soft, relatively large bill, and soft bulging bumps above the nostrils. They rest on their stomachs and hold the neck upright with the head resting between the shoulders and the bill pointing forwards.

Nidicolous young always have a complete and camouflaging down. The pinions grow very quickly, and some young can fly short distances at only eight days of age.

Caring Properly for Nidicolous Young

Unfledged nidicolous birds need a surrogate nest. You can make one but placing hay, straw, or soft rags into a cardboard box or a plant pot. Polystyrene boxes are also most suitable because they keep in heat well. Make a hollow in the nest material which is deep enough that the bird will not be able to fall out of it. You should not use woolen thread or wood shavings or the like, as they may get wound around the bird's throat and strangle it or the young might try to feed on them, swallow a never-ending thread, and choke to death. Old and empty bird nests that you might come across outside are also unsuitable as they are usually full of mites and other pests.

In the case of larger nidicolous young— birds of prey—the nesting material should be coarser. It can be made with smaller and larger twigs, just as a natural nest.

All young birds will be harmed by damp and drafts. It is not advisable to put the nest and its inhabitants on the floor or near the window, even if it is closed. There should be a corner somewhere in the room which is not in the draft between the door and the window, where the nest can be put in a handy position.

Unfeathered young need a constant supply of warm air. As soon as the body is covered in feathers this is no longer necessary. The temperature must not exceed 100°F (38°C) and should not go below 86°F (30°C). Electric pillows, infra-red beams, or a 30-watt bulb will provide the heat required.

Keep a constant check on the temperature. If the bird tears open its bill, stretches its head and neck, or cries out, then it is too

Raising Foundlings

warm. As soon as a bird wishes to leave the nest, you will need a perch which is right for its size, that is, the span of its toes. Shortly afterwards the bird's natural urge to move will become evident. It will want to walk, hop, and make its first attempts at flying. Now you will need to look for a cage or an aviary for it where it can stay for awhile.

Surrogate nest for nidicolous birds: a flowerpot well-stuffed with straw.

Nidifugous young are able to walk only a few hours after hatching. This means they need more space than birds which leave the nest late. Ideally they should be kept in a part of the room which has plenty of daylight and sun, which is partitioned off from the rest of the room with a few boards. They will need a surface area of at least 1 square yard (1 m²); more as they grow larger. In the beginning they will try to get out of the enclosed space, as they do not encounter any insurmountable vertical barriers in their natural habitat. The barrier should not be made of glass, as the birds can see through it and constantly will try to get through it, too. In the case of wire barriers they may damage their bills and hurt their heads.

Then again, the space should not be too large or the birds may have problems finding the heat source when they are cold. Here, too, the space can be heated with an infra-red beam (60-100 watt) or a bulb (60-100 watt), which should be hung over the pen. The birds can then choose the part of the area which has the most suitable temperature for them.

Most nidifugous birds not only feed independently from the outset but also drink, and many species are even fond of bathing. Place the food and water containers in the centre of the pen. If you put them around the edges the birds will be trampling through them constantly as they move around the sides, and the food and water will very quickly get dirty.

The chicks of wild fowl, such as pheasants or partridges, are able to fly after only a few days. Their primaries develop very quickly. Ideally, the pen should be covered with a fine wire or stretchable plastic netting.

Once their bodies are covered in feathers, there is no need for additional heating. If the weather is fine they can be put into an aviary during the day, where they can also be kept should you decide not to set them free.

Feeding Nidicolous Young

The food should be suited to the age and the species of the bird or it will not be well received and the breeding will be a failure from the start.

First a word on feeding techniques: Some of these birds will take the food from you with their bills; others will open their mouths and wait to have the food popped in. This is known as "gaping" (see colour photos, page

Raising Foundlings

38). Birds of prey and owls do not do this, but all others do, except doves, whose feeding habits will be dealt with separately (see page 45). Place the food in the bill as far back as possible so that it can be swallowed easily. Older chicks are able to move the food from the front of the bill to the back with their tongues and do not need any extra help from us. Very small birds cannot do this and the food will fall out again. Blunt-ended pincers should be used for feeding in this way.

Older chicks, which have known their own parents and are suspicious of anything unusual, at first will not usually gape. In this case you will have to gently force the bill open and drop in the food. The best way to do this is to take the bird in your left hand, hold the head between your thumb and index finger, and prop open the bill with a soft wooden stick at the side of the mouth (as illustrated on page 45). After a short time the bird will start gaping automatically. You will

Suitable accommodation for nidifugous chicks: a cardboard box or crate with bowls for food and water and a heating source.

need to take care not to give the bird pieces of food which are too large for it to swallow or it may choke on them.

Feeding the species which take the food themselves is less complicated. You will only need to hold the food in front of a bird of prey or an owl's beak and it will take and swallow without any assistance. Even these species may well resist feeding at first. Sometimes stroking the corner of the bill with the food or rubbing it around the edges will help. The bird will then snap it up.

What do you feed which bird? **Birds of prey and owls** eat animal fodder; the meat of warm-blooded animals and insects. The most natural food would be mice, as that is their main food source in the wild. If mice are not available then you can feed them raw lean meat of slaughtered animals. Heart is highly recommendable. In the long term, however, a pure-meat diet is not desirable.

Birds of prey and owls form fur balls in their stomachs (see page 48). To do this they need to have swallowed hair, feathers, and small bones first. If they are to be fed a pure-meat diet, you should occasionally wrap the meat in hair or feathers.

All young birds raised in captivity will need supplements of calcium. Your veterinarian can advise you.

The young bird—and this is true for all species—will let you know how often and how much you should feed it. If it is satisfied, then it will not gape and will not accept any more food. If it is hungry, it will gape and beg. It is better for the bird to feed it small amounts often rather than large amounts rarely.

Members of the **crow family** can be fed meat, low-fat curds mixed with oat flakes, or soft foods and insects. You should not in-

Raising Foundlings

clude large amounts of feathers and hair, though a little mouse fur does not cause any harm.

Young **doves** are fed on crop milk by their parents. It consists of the first layer of the inside of the crop mixed with pre-digested grain and fodder. The young get the food by putting their beaks inside their parent's beaks, which then regurgitates the pulp. It will be difficult for you to emulate this. But you can make your own substitute pulp by mixing together previously soaked bread (white or brown) with oat flakes, soaked millet and wheat, boiled egg yolk, and a little mealworm. Feed it to the bird between three fingers.

If a chick balks at gaping, then it will need to be helped to feed.

Small song birds and soft-food eaters are not easy to raise. Their natural diet is earthworms (especially for thrushes), all manner of insects, spiders, insect larvae, and insect eggs. It is possible to find food for individual young of the smaller species. You catch flies in fly traps: Put a paper funnel on top of a preserving jar containing some rotting meat. The flies, attracted by the smell of the meat, will crawl inside and be unable to get out again. To prevent the flies from coming into contact with the meat and taking on a carrion smell, which many birds do not like, cover the meat with fine gauze or blotting paper.

Gnats, moths, and other nocturnal insects can be caught in similar ways. Instead of using rotting meat as bait, put a light bulb over the funnel. The insect will fly towards the source of light, bang into it, and fall into the glass.

When feeding insects you have caught yourself you should watch out for insects with striking warning colours—black and red or yellow and red. Nor should you feed them stinging insects, such as bees and wasps, unless you remove the sting first. The bird will react to food that it does not want by shaking its head and trying to get rid of whatever it is you have put in its bill. Do be watchful for such signs.

As a substitute for live food you can mix low-fat curds with soft food, boiled egg, finely chopped raw heart, or lean minced meat. The chances for a successful rearing will be enhanced by occasionally including in the diet some skinned mealworms (from a pet shop), pupae (from under stones in the garden), and the odd spider or hairless caterpillar. A good pet shop will stock ready-made food for fledglings and will give help and advice with breeding.

Young domestic fowl initially eat more meat than grain. They need plenty of soft food, pheasant-rearing fodder, mealworms, and insects. Meadow plankton—small animals which you can collect by passing a butterfly net over tall grass—is a wonderful natural foodstuff. Even if you can only give it to the chicks very occasionally, it will do wonders for them. Although the chicks mainly feed on animals initially, you can give them small seeds, such as millet, poppy, bloom, or hemp, and oat flakes. Sooner or later the chicks will adjust. You should also remember to give them drinking water, of course, and provide them with a little sand to take a sand bath in. You can buy bird sand in pet shops and department stores. The young can then swallow small stones, which will help them to break down the seeds and hard outer skeletons of insects.

When Is the Foundling Fully Fledged?

A bird is independent once it can fly and find and eat its own food independently.

Birds learn to fly at a certain stage, even if not always with a great deal of "technical ability". Things are slightly different when it comes to finding food. In captivity the birds are used to finding their food in a particular place. When set free they have to hunt for it themselves. This is not an adjustment all species find easy to make.

When releasing hand-reared birds, you should take care of the following:
• When the bird is independent, gradually wean it from its rearer, place it in as large an aviary as possible, and pay little attention to it—whilst still providing it with food and water, of course. Only release it when it is in peak condition (including its plumage). Release it at a time when there is plenty of food available in the wild, between June and August. This will give the bird enough time until autumn (or winter, in the case of those which stay) to fully accustom itself to a life in the wild. Release the bird into an environment that suits its species: a forest bird in a forest, a duck near a pond.
• Small birds, which have a generous supply of food sources in the summer months, usually have few problems surviving. The same is true of domestic fowl, which feed on green fodder as well as insects and seeds.

The most interesting way for the rearer and the safest way for the bird is to make a very gradual transition from hand-rearing to living in the wild. I once tried it with a very tame hand-reared blackbird. Once it could fly I left the window open, and it would often make short excursions into the outside world but always return to me at first. In time it stayed away for longer and longer stretches, even finding its own food, occasionally. After about a week it was entirely independent and thoroughly at home in its new environment. Finally it disappeared, never to be seen again.

Winter Visitors and Breeding Birds

Things Worth Knowing About Our Birds

A short excursion into *bird biology* should help us understand the habits of birds even better. Of course I cannot live up to the expectations of an expert, but with the help of the characteristic features I would like to explain, in a few words, what a bird is to those who are not—or not yet—to be found among the "experts" (see Further Reading, page 69).

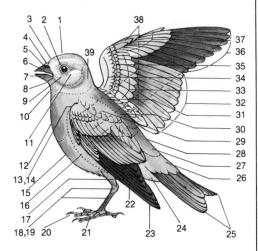

1 Crown, 2 Eye ring, 3 Forehead, 4 Cere, 5 Nostril, 6 Upper mandible, 7 Lower mandible, 8 Chin, 9 Cheek, 10 Throat, 11 Ear coverts, 12 Breast, 13 Shoulder, 14 Bend of wing, 15 Abdomen, 16 Flank, 17 Tarsus, 18 Heel, 19 Foot, 20 Claws, 21 Toes, 22 Cloaca, 23 Primary feathers, 24 Under tail coverts, 25 Outer tail feathers, 26 Upper tail coverts, 27 Rump, 28 Lower back, 29 Scapular, 30 Back, 31 Upper back, 32 Secondary feathers, 33 Greater secondary coverts, 34 Marginal coverts, 35 Medium and lesser secondary coverts, 36 Primary feathers, 37 Greater Primary coverts, 38 Upper wing coverts, 39 Nape

Birds are *vertebrates* but are different from other vertebrates as they have *feathers*. The feathers are made of a horny substance, like the scales of reptiles, from which birds are probably descended. In birds, horny scales are only found on the legs. The bony part of the beak is also covered by a layer of horn. Birds, like mammals, are *warm-blooded* animals: they produce and regulate their body temperature via the circulatory system, regardless of the environmental temperature. Of all living organisms, birds have the highest body temperature, ranging on average between 104 and 113°F. By using their feathers they can largely even out external changes in temperature. When a bird ruffles its feathers a great deal of air is trapped between them. This air is then warmed by the body and forms an insulating layer between the body and the air outside. When a bird becomes too warm, it compresses its feathers tightly and the insulating layer of air is expelled. A bird cannot sweat, as it has no sweat glands. Should it still feel too warm, it opens its beak and evaporates moisture from its throat. The *heart*, the blood system's pumping station, is larger than that of mammals. It also works harder, producing more output per heartbeat at a higher frequency. The number of heartbeats per minute for the adult chicken may vary from 250 to 400; for the house sparrow, 400 to 800; for the goldfinch, as many as 925; and for the blue-throated humming bird—the maximum avian heart rate recorded to date—1,260 beats per minute. The heart is like a motor and is permanently in use. It requires constant fueling if it is not to stop.

Its fuel is food. The food and feeding process of a bird are as multifaceted as the world of birds as a whole, but the saying

Winter Visitors and Breeding Birds

"Bird eat or die" applies to all birds. None can go without food for a length of time. Reserves are fast exhausted. A small bird can die after only a few hours without food. It has to eat the equivalent of one third of its body weight every day, and even more when it is cold outside. Some bird species have a crop in which the food can be stored and pre-digested. With others it goes straight into the stomach. Digestion, the breaking up of the food by the digestive juices and its integration into the metabolism, happens very fast. Indigestible scraps of food generally reappear very soon. They are either excreted, generally in pulpy or fluid form, through the *cloaca*, the orifice used for passing urine and droppings and for laying eggs, or regurgitated through the gullet and spat out. These scraps, made up of hairs, feathers, bone fragments, and the hard horny exoskeleton parts of insects, are spat out mostly in the form of small balls or "little sausages" and are called waste pellets or furballs.

The bird's *lung* also has a special structure. Inhaled air not only enters it but some of it goes through the lung into air pockets which stretch out form it into different parts of the body. This ensures a better exchange of gases in the lung. At the same time the air pockets work in a way similar to the radiator in a car, especially between the breast muscles, which have to perform a tremendous amount of work when flying. Birds are primarily eye-centred animals and possess outstanding *eyesight*. Their *hearing* is good too, as evidenced by the multitude of calls and songs they use, which would be pointless if they could not be perceived by others. The sense of *smell*, however, is only slightly developed in most species. They can taste, however. The sense of *taste* as well as the sense of *touch* are of great importance when searching for food and eating. One often wonders how skillful birds can be with their *beaks*. Seed-eating birds are past masters at using the beak to husk grain. The *toes*, too, are not only suitable for walking and hopping or holding onto boughs. They are just as good for holding food while it is being worked on by the beak.

All birds lay *eggs*, out of which the young hatch. There is no species of bird that gives birth to live young. Almost all birds hatch their eggs themselves and look after the young afterwards. Only nest scroungers like our native cookoo leave the hatching of their eggs to so-called host birds. The following descriptions of the winter visitors and nesters are classified according to species.

Brief Descriptions of Birds: Appearance, Call, Behaviour, Habitat, Breeding, and Feeding

European buzzard   Colour plate page 56 (*Buteo buteo*) 20–22 inches (51–56 cm) Family: Accipitridae

The plumage is of variable colours, ranging from dark brown to almost white, in both sexes. The wingspan is between 46 and 54 inches. In flight it has wide wings and a short, fan-like tail. It often flies clumsily and slowly, sometimes in a heavy jolting way. It also frequently glides in circles. Voice: cat-like mewing "pee-oo" or "hee-oo". It often sits on lookouts, such as telegraph poles or fence posts when hunting for small animals. It breeds throughout Europe, except in the far north. Its large, flat nest is built in forests in the tops of tall trees. The breeding season is from the end of March to the end of May,

Winter Visitors and Breeding Birds

two to three eggs; the incubation period is 33–35 days. The young are insessorial birds, wear a white, downy plumage, and are fledged after 40–50 days.

The buzzard feeds on small mammals (mainly mice), young birds, and lizards and also larger insects. In winter it also eats carrion. In long winters, with a thick blanket of snow, you can feed the buzzard with scraps of meat (lung, liver, or heart) at ''waste grounds'', which can be created near free-standing trees in parks and larger gardens. Because they are hungry the birds will grow quite trusting. Distribution: Europe, Asia.

Kestrel   Colour plate page 38 (young bird)
(Falco tinnunculus) 14 inches (34 cm)
Family: Falconidae

Small, brown falcon with a long tail of even width from root to tip. Male has a grey head, rust-red and black-flecked back, grey tail, and black tail bar. The female is rust-red, except for the primaries. Both sexes have a yellowish, dark-spotted underside. Wing span: 31 inches (75 cm); flight is hasty with even beats. Call: especially at breeding time, frequent shrill ''kee-kee-kee'' sounds. When hunting for prey it spies from a high perch or hovers above. The kestrel—one of Europe's most common birds of prey—lives anywhere from coastal regions to mountain ranges, except for closed woodlands. It also lives in cities. It normally does not build its own nest but nests in abandoned crow, magpie, or pigeon nests on cliff ledges, or in trees, church towers, and other high buildings. Breeds from March to early April (later in the north), four to six eggs; incubation period, 27–31 days. The young are nidicolous (they stay in the nest a long time), have white down, and are fledged after 27–38 days.

It lives on mice and other small vertebrates and insects. Kestrels cannot find sufficient food when there is heavy snowfall. They can be fed on lean, salt-free scraps of meat. Distribution: Europe, Asia, Africa.

Barn owl
(Tyto alba) 14 inches (34 cm)
Family: Owl (Strigidae)

Of all native owls the barn owl has the most distinctive heart-shaped face, framing the eyes and beak. The eyes are dark. The underside is light brown with fine dark spots (in the Central European variety) or white and sparsely spotted in the southern continental and British variety. Topside is grey with gold-brown spots. Sexes alike. Call: screeching, purring, and hissing sounds. In the days when there were still lots of old barns in villages, with open church towers and farmhouses with ''owlholes'', the barn owl was a common bird. Now it has become very rare in England; as its nesting places have been taken from it. (The current total is estimated to be between 4,500 and 9,000 pairs.) Active at night; flight soundless due to the soft plumage. The barn owl chooses

Making artificial nest holes for barn owls is sensible but very difficult. You should seek professional advice.

dark corners of barns and old buildings to breed in, as well as holes in walls and—more rarely—in trees. Breeding period from March to October, four to six eggs. Nesting period, 44–67 days. The young can fly after about 65 days.

Feed on mice, particularly shrews, reptiles, and larger types of insects. In harsh and snowy winters the barn owls suffer food shortages as the mice stay under the snow. They will then accept laboratory mice (see pages 17 and 18). Distribution: Europe, southern Asia, Australia, Africa, North and South America.

Long-eared owl   Colour photo page 38
(young bird)
(*Asio otus*) 15 inches (36 cm)
Family: Owl (Strigidae)

This owl looks thin when observed sitting in a tree. It deliberately makes itself look thin and therefore less noticeable. It has distinctive ear tufts on the head, orange-yellow eyes, and a clearly delineated face; otherwise buff coloured, yellow-brown with darker markings. Sexes alike. Call: warning call "ooek"; at breeding time the male utters a muffled "hoo", the female a hoarse "vaya" or "jaya", the young a high-pitched "feed". Long-eared owls are still relatively common. They live in open landscapes with scattered trees and copses. During the day they hide in high trees (often beside the trunk) and only become active at dusk. In winter, long-eared owls form sleeping communes. You can observe several to a tree, to which they will always return to rest unless disturbed. They breed in trees, not building their own nests but using abandoned crow and magpie nests. Breeding period: April to June, four to seven eggs; incubation period, 27–28 days. The grey-white young leave the

eyrie at about 3 weeks and perch in neighbouring trees and bushes, unable to fly. They are fed by the adult birds. They can fly after about 34 days.

Feed mainly on mice and voles, as well as smaller birds, insects, and lizards. In harsh and snowy winters they can be fed on mice (see pages 17 and 18). Distribution: Europe, Asia, northern Africa, North America.

Tawny owl
(*Strix aluco*) 15 inches (38 cm)
Family: Owl (Strigidae)

Ranging from rust-brown to grey-brown in colour, stout looking with no ear tufts and with dark blue eyes which may appear black. Sexes alike. Call: in autumn and spring its territorial call is the striking "hoo-hoo-hoo-hooooo"; in autumn (and especially from the young), a hoarse "ke-wick". The tawny owl is one of our most common birds of prey and prefers old deciduous trees and parklands with old trees but is also to be found in cities. It likes the sun but only becomes active at night. It spends the whole year in its breeding territory. Tawny owls breed in wall or tree holes. Breeding period, February to May, three to five eggs; incubation period 28–30 days. The down of the young is white-grey. The young can fly after about 45 days.

Feed on mice and other small mammals up to the size of squirrels, frogs, large insects, and birds. More rarely they eat worms. As it hunts birds the tawny owl is less dependent on our help than other native owls. Distribution: Europe, Southeast Asia. It has never been recorded in Ireland.

Partridge
(*Perdix perdix*) 12 inches (30 cm)
Family: Partridge (Phasianidae)

The partridge is a stocky, short-tailed common partridge with grey-brown, dark

Winter Visitors and Breeding Birds

brown spotted and striped plumage, and a reddish brown head. Males have a chestnut-coloured horseshoe marking on the stomach which is either missing or very faint in females. Otherwise the sexes are alike. Call: a grating "keevit", especially in spring. Partridges live in open cultivated country at low and moderate altitudes. In winter they join together in so-called coveys. In summer they live in pairs and family groupings. The nest is a well-hidden scrape in the ground. Breeding period from end of April until beginning of June; 10–20 greenish grey eggs: incubation period, about 25 days. The young are nidifugous (they leave the nest after a short time). They have a yellowish brown down and can fly after about 12 days.

Feed on both insects, worms, vegetation, and seeds. The chicks especially require a great deal of animal food in the first few weeks. In harsh winters partridges move closer to villages and the edges of towns. Feeding boxes should be at ground level and covered. They will eat grain and seeds. Distribution: Europe, western Asia.

Pheasant   Colour photo page 56
(*Phasianus colchicus*) male: 30–35 inches (66–89 cm), female: 21–25 inches, (53–63 cm)
Family: Partridge (Phasianidae)

The male has a strikingly colourful iridescent plumage with a greenish head and very long tail; around the eyes there is a pure red patch of skin. The female is sandy-coloured with dark speckles with a considerably shorter tail and without the red patch. Call: the male crows "kor-kok"; the mating call is a cackling "ker-ker-kre". The pheasant originally came from Asia but has been introduced into many countries. It lives in open parkland, more rarely in woodland.

Mainly to be seen on the ground but flies off when disturbed; sleeps at night in trees. It breeds on the ground (the female only) in thick vegetation. Breeding period from the beginning of April until the beginning of May, 8–12 eggs; incubation period, 23–25 days. The young leave the nest early and have a yellowish down with dark flecks; they can fly after only 12 days and are capable of surviving entirely unaided after 70–80 days.

Feed mainly on plants, berries, fruit, and seeds but also on insects, worms, and molluscs; in winter they feed mainly on plants and seeds. Pheasants will only survive hard, snowy winters if they are fed at "pheasant dens" (see page 12). Distribution: Europe, Asia.

Collared turtle dove
(*Streptopelia decaocto*) 11 inches (28 cm)
Family: Dove (Columbidae)

A very pale sand-coloured dove with a black-and-white trimmed half-collar. Sexes alike. Call: a constant trisyllabic "coo-cooo-cuh"; in flight a nasal "neeh". This century has seen the collared dove spread quickly from the Balkans over Central Europe. In England, the first pair bred in Norfolk in 1955. By 1972, the doves were widespread through lowland Britain and much of Ireland. By 1977, they had been officially declared a pest species and were put on Schedule II of the Protection of Birds Acts. They live almost exclusively amongst human settlements, especially where grain is available. Outside the breeding season collared doves are very gregarious and often come together in large droves to particular sleeping spots. Their flat nests are built in evergreen trees or amongst ivy. Breeding period,

Winter Visitors and Breeding Birds

March to October (breeding two to four times a year), two eggs; incubation period, 13–16 days. The young leave the nest late and are fed on crop milk, as is common among doves. (The milk is a pulp secreted by a gland in the crop.) Later this is mixed with grain and vegetation. Nesting period, 14–20 days.

Feed mainly on seeds, berries, and parts of plants. As collared doves are not very shy they will also feed on waste products from silos, stables, and farmyards. In winter they are especially dependent on being fed by us, primarily on seeds; they will readily use feeding boxes but generally search the ground for food. Distribution: Europe, southern Asia.

Great spotted woodpecker

(*Dendrocopos major*) 9 inches (23 cm)
Family: Woodpecker (Picidae)

The plumage is a highly contrasting black and white with red undertail feathers and a red patch on the back of the head (missing in the female); the young have a red patch on the forehead. The quills of the tail feathers are used for support when the bird is climbing along trees and branches with the head held back.

Call: when excited a repeated "kik"; mating call is a harsh "rehrehreh". The territorial and mating signal is a drumming noise produced by tapping the bill on dead boughs or, occasionally, on gutters and weather vanes. The great spotted woodpecker—our most common woodpecker—is at home in both small and larger woodlands, mainly mixed woods, but is also often to be seen in parklands and gardens. The male and female excavate a hole in a tree (often in a dead elm or birch) for their young. Breeding period, May to June, five to seven eggs; incubation

period, 12–13 days. The young leave the nest late and are fully fledged at about 20 days.

In summer great spotted woodpeckers feed mainly on insects and their larvae, which they find in bark or channels of trees. These channels are widened with their beaks and the larvae are winkled out with the very long and barbed tongues of the birds. In winter and autumn they will also eat nuts, beechnuts, and seeds from conifers. In winter they readily come to feeding stations and eat berries, plums, nuts, sunflower seeds, peach stones, and even suet. Distribution: Europe, Asia, northwest Africa.

Skylark

(*Alauda arrensis*) 6¾ inches (17 cm)
Family: Lark (Alaudidae)

A fairly short-tailed, stout-looking umber lark with black stripes. Its plumage is very inconspicuous. The outer tail feathers are white; the crown feathers are often ruffled. Sexes alike. Call: A quavering "chir-r-r-up". Its song is extremely melodic and is mixed with imitations of various other birds' songs, usually delivered while fluttering high above the ground, often for several minutes.

Skylarks prefer cultivated lands with sparse or no vegetation. On the outskirts of towns, railway sidings, sports grounds, or even in city centres they will seek out building sites and other similar locations. They are quite trusting. They like to run on the ground to look for food. Their walk is a tripping, almost rolling motion of quick steps. The nest is a flat hollow in the ground, loosely woven with straw, blades of grass, and fine roots. Breeding period April to July (mostly breeding twice a year), three to five eggs; incubation period, 14 days. The young

Winter Visitors and Breeding Birds

leave the nest before fully fledged and are fed by both parents.

Feed on insects, small seeds, and greenery. In winter skylarks will search for anything edible, often coming right up to houses. At feeding stations they will feed on small seeds, oats, and bread crumbs. Distribution: Europe, Asia, northern Africa.

House martin

(*Delichon urbica*) 5 inches (13 cm)
Family: Swallow (Hirundinidae)

Male and female colouring alike; upper side is blue-black with white rump, underside white. The tail is clearly forked but without the long streamers of the swallow. Call: "trr", "chirrp", or "brii"; alarm note a high-pitched "tseeep". Its song is gentle chatting and chirrup. Like the swallow, the house martin seeks the proximity of human beings. They live in settlements, villages, and cities (surveys in London show a steady increase of martin colonies). House martins live in small or large colonies with up to 200 nests built on the walls of houses. The nests are made of gobbets of mud with a single hole in the upper corner. They will also accept artificial nests (see page 34). Breeding period, May to September (breeding two or three times a year), four to five eggs; incubation period, 13–14 days. Nesting period, 16–23 days.

Feed exclusively on insects caught on the wing. House martins migrate, often in the company of swallows, to their winter quarters south of the Sahara in October and return in April. Distribution: Europe, Asia, northwest Africa.

Swallow

(*Hirundo rustica*) 7½ inches (19 cm)
Family: Swallow (Hirundidae)

The swallow has very long outer tail feathers, which makes the tail appear forked. Upper sides and neck ring are blue-black; throat and forehead are red. Underside white. Male and female colouring alike. Call: "tswitt, tswit"; alarm note "tsink, tsink". The song is a rapid twittering with a purring sound at the end. The swallow lives almost exclusively in the vicinity of human settlements. In rural areas in particular they will find sufficient food from farmyards, stables, and marshes. They are not shy and nest mostly in buildings, particularly stables. The saucer-shaped nest, open at the top, is made of pellets of mud and damp soil mixed with grass and saliva, and lined with feathers; artificial nests will be accepted (see page 34). Breeding period, May to September (breeding twice or three times a year), four to six eggs; incubation period, 13–18 days. Nesting period, 20–22 days.

Feed mainly on insects caught skillfully on the wing. Only in periods of very heavy rains can flying insects be snapped up from their resting places on stalks. The swallow migrates to Africa in October and returns between the end of March and early April. Distribution: Europe, Asia, North Africa, North America.

Pied wagtail or **white wagtail**

(*Motacilla alba*) 7 inches (18 cm)
Family: Wagtails (Motacillidae)

The males of this family have long and constantly wagging tails and a highly contrasting black-and-white colouration; the females are somewhat paler. The crown, chin, throat, and upper breast are black; forehead, chin, and underside are white; back, light grey. Call: "tschizzick". Its song is a high-pitched twittering. Lives in open country, often though not exclusively near water. They like to build their nests with protection from above on buildings, under roof beams, or in sheds or a cavity. They will readily accept artificial cavities. Breeding period, April to August, five to six eggs; incubation period, 12–14 days. Nesting period, 14–15 days.

Feed on insects and spiders, which they find on the ground and chase with fast, tripping steps and sometimes catch in short burst of flight. Many pied wagtails remain in Britain during the winter, although some migrate to Mediterranean areas in autumn and return in March. Distribution: Europe, Asia, northwest Africa.

Waxwing   Colour photo page 55
(*Bombycilla garrulus*) 7 inches (18 cm)
Family: Waxwing (Bombycillidae)

A bird with characteristic pastel markings, about the size of a starling, with a reddish brown crest, black throat, and black around the eyes. Upper side is reddish brown, lighter on the stomach. Tail feathers are black with yellow bar; wings brown-black with two white flecks and red markings on the tips of the secondaries. Call: "sirrrr" or "deeuu"; its song is a high trill and chatter (though seldom heard in winter). Depending on the weather conditions this visitor from the Far North can arrive in large or small numbers in November or December. They gather on berry-bearing bushes. They are not in the slightest shy! They build their nests in birch or pine forests when they return to their breeding grounds in March and early April. They breed in loose-knit colonies. Breeding period, May to June, four to five eggs; incubation period, 12–15 days, nesting period, 14–16 days. They feed mainly on berries; in summer they also hunt gnats and other insects. They sometimes appear at feeding stations in winter but only if they can not find berries. Distribution: northern Europe, northern Asia, North America.

Hedge sparrow or **dunnock**   Colour photo page 28
(*Prunella modularis*) 5¾ inches (14.5 cm)
Family: Accentors (Prunellidae)

This small, dainty, and yet very inconspicuous bird is often confused with the house sparrow as it bustles about with them on feeding tables. Its beak, however, is much thinner and sharper than a sparrow's, and the way it moves is also different. Sexes alike. Call: a high-pitched whistling "tseep" or a rapid sequence of "tsee-tsee". The melodic, rapid twittering song is only heard in spring and summer. Hedge sparrows can be seen almost everywhere in parks and gardens, even on the Scottish moors or on the Hebridean Islands, but they live well hidden in thick bushes and spend much of their time on the ground. The nest is mainly made from thick twigs of pine trees and other dense shrubs. Breeding period, April to July (mostly breeding twice a year), four to five eggs; incubation period, 13 days. Nesting period, 13–14 days.

Feed mainly on insects but also on fine seeds and small berries. Many hedge sparrows migrate to west or southwest Europe in autumn, but some do winter here, often joined by birds from the Continent, and are then to be observed regularly at feeding places, feeding on small seeds, oat flakes, berries, raisins, and small pieces of fruit. Distribution: Europe and Asia Minor.

Common and rare visitors to feeding stations. Above left: Crossbill. Above right: Greenfinch. Centre left: Hawfinch. Centre right: Waxwing. Below left: Brambling—male with winter plumage. Below right: Male chaffinch.

Winter Visitors and Breeding Birds

Spotted flycatcher   Colour photo page 37
(*Muscicapa striata*) 5½ inches (14 cm)
Family: Flycatcher (Muscicapidae)

The spotted flycatcher is not a particularly rare bird but its inconspicuous colouring means that it often escapes notice. The upper side is grey-brown, the underside whitish with dark streaks on the head and breast. Sexes alike. Call: "tzee" or "psst"; alarm call "whee-tucc-tucc". Its song is a quiet and thin twittering and whispering. In summer the spotted flycatcher lives in beech woods, parks, and gardens. Mostly they sit bolt upright on high lookout posts and swoop down to catch insects on the wing. When perching they will often jerk their wings. The nest, made of moss, hair, and feathers, is built in niches, cavities, under rafters and eaves, or similar places. Spotted flycatchers will also make use of artificial nests or cavities. Breeding period, May to July, four to six eggs; incubation period, 12–14 days. Nesting period, 10–14 days.

They feed almost exclusively on flying insects. Spotted flycatchers migrate to central and southern Africa at the end of August and return in early May. Distribution: Europe, Asia, northwest Africa.

Pied flycatcher
(*Ficedula hypoleuca*) 5 inches (13 cm)
Family: Flycatcher (Muscicapidae)

The male of the central European species is generally a grey-brown colour; in the north and south, black; forehead and underside white with white bar on wing. Females paler, without white patch on forehead. Call: "whit"; song a bisyllabic "wooti-wooti". Pied flycatchers live in deciduous and mixed

Above: Pheasants feeding. Below: Buzzard at the "waste ground" (meat scraps on wooden post).

woods, parks, and gardens. They perch quite stiffly on the branch. Pied flycatchers breed in tree holes or nest boxes. The female builds the nest from leaves, fern, fibres, and stalks. Breeding period, May to June, five to eight eggs; incubation period, 12–16 days. Nesting period, 12–17 days.

From their lookout posts they snatch up insects—their main foodstuffs—on the wing. In late summer they will also eat berries. They leave in August/September and return in April/May. Distribution: Europe, western Asia, northwest Africa.

The **collared flycatcher** (*Ficedula albicollis*) is a close relative. It has a wide collar ring and is a resident of Southern and Western Europe. Its way of life is very similar to that of the pied flycatcher.

Black redstart
(*Phoenicurus ochruros*) 5½ inches (14 cm)
Family: Flycatcher (Muscicapidae)

The body is an ash-grey colour with soot-black throat and breast; the rump and tail feathers are chestnut. The female is a more uniform dark grey-brown with a chestnut tail. Call: "hwee-tucc-tucc"; song: a staccato, high-pitched warble to start with, a few compressed notes, and then a final "widee-tree-tree". Originally black redstarts were residents of sea cliffs; nowadays they are at home in stone quarries, villages, and towns of lowland areas. They breed in rocky crevices, holes in walls, and on roof beams and will readily take to nest boxes. Breeding period, April to July (breeding twice a year), five to six eggs; incubation period, 13 days. Nesting period, 12–17 days. The young resemble the females but are more flecked.

Feed on insects, spiders, and berries. Black redstarts migrate to Western Europe

Winter Visitors and Breeding Birds

and Mediterranean countries in late October and return to their breeding grounds in March. Distribution: Europe, Asia, northwest Africa.

Redstart
(*Phoenicurus phoenicurus*) 5½ inches (14 cm)
Family: Flycatcher (Muscicapidae)

The male redstart is more strikingly coloured than the black redstart. It has black cheeks, a black throat, a white spot on the forehead, a reddish breast, and a yellowish stomach; the upper side is slate-grey; rump and tail are a fiery chestnut. Females are brownish with a light underside. Call: "wheet-tucc-tucc". The song is a short and melodic "hooeet". A striking behaviour pattern of the redstart is its frequent bowing and splaying of the tail. It breeds in open and mixed woods, gardens, parks, and orchards. The nest is found in cavities and is made of grass, roots, and moss; they will readily take to nest boxes. Breeding period, May to July (breeding twice a year), five to seven eggs; incubation period, 12–17 days; nesting period, 12–14 days. The young are similar to those of the black redstart.

Feed on insects, spiders, and berries. The redstart returns from its winter quarters somewhat later than its relatives, in late March. It migrates no later than October. Distribution: Europe, Asia, northwest Africa.

Robin   Colour photo on page 9
(*Erithacus rubecula*) 5½ inches (14 cm)
Family: Flycatcher (Muscicapidae)

The robin, with its olive-brown upper side and red breast, must be one of the best known of the smaller birds. Usually rather stout with big, black eyes. Sexes alike. Call: alarm note a sharp "tic-tic-tic". Its song is a melodic rippling sound sung late into the evening, usually from a high vantage point. Found in parks, gardens, and woods with dense vegetation. Hops about looking for food. Its behaviour shows few traces of shyness. The nest may be built on the ground at the edges of ditches or in tree holes or niches in walls. The nest is made by the female from soft vegetation. Breeding period, April to July, four to six eggs; incubation period, 13 days. Nesting period, 12–15 days. The young have a brownish, lightly speckled early plumage which camouflages them well.

In summer the robin feeds mainly on insects, spiders, and worms. A portion of our robins migrate in autumn to southern, Mediterranean countries; the majority winter in their breeding quarters. Robins, then, are frequent visitors to feeding places, where they feed on small seeds, squashed nuts, oats, and suet. To the robin, mildew is a special treat. Even less shy than in the summer, they are hardly to be disturbed at all at feeding places. But they do not always have it easy holding their ground against the stronger tits, finches, and sparrows. Distribution: Europe, western Asia, northwest Africa.

Blackbird   Colour photo back cover
(*Turdus merula*) 10 inches (25 cm)
Family: Flycatcher (Muscicapidae)

The males are jet black with a yellow beak and eye ring; the females are brown. Call: warning call a shrill "teeks-teeks-teeks" and a deep "took-took", a loud clamouring sound, and, when being attacked in the air, a long drawn-out "tseee". Their song is one of the most beautiful and melodic of our birds. Along with the house sparrow and the pigeon, the blackbird—also known as the

Winter Visitors and Breeding Birds

black thrush—is known to all, living, as it does, in villages and cities the whole year round. Its true and original home is the forest; but the blackbird is becoming more and more "citified". In the forest the nest is built in trees; in the city it is often built under roof beams and balconies, in window boxes, or in holes in a wall. It is made of grass, roots, and other plant material, sometimes held together with mud or damp soil. Breeding period, March to July (breeding up to four times a year in the cities), three to five eggs; incubation, about 13 days. The young usually leave the nest before they can fly and spend a few days hopping about on the ground. This makes them easy prey for cats, and cars are a big danger.

Blackbirds usually search for food on the ground. They are especially fond of earthworms, which they pull out of the soil with their beaks. But in autumn they will also eat large amounts of berries, nuts, and fruit. They have also been known to eat shrews, lizards, newts, and even trout fry. City blackbirds are very unassuming and will accept bits of bread and pigeon feed. Some blackbirds fly south in the winter; but for the most part city blackbirds spend their winter in their breeding quarter. They are regular visitors to feeding places and will eat small seeds, oat flakes, bits of bread, berries, and fruit. They may well "occupy" a bird table with considerable tenacity before finally giving way to other birds. Distribution: Europe, Asia, northwest Africa.

Fieldfare   Colour photos pages 10 and 28
(*Turdus pilaris*) 10 inches (25.5 cm)
Family: Flycatcher (Muscicapidae)

A thrush with highly contrasting markings. Head, neck, and rump are chestnut brown, as are the wings; tail and secondaries dark; throat and breast yellowish brown with dark speckles. Call: an undistinguished chattering and twittering sound. In earlier times, the fieldfare bred only in the Taigas and on the Nordic moors. Then it migrated farther and farther south, and now it inhabits the whole of Central Europe. It is a gregarious bird and lives in flocks of up to 200 birds, usually accompanied by starlings, redwings, and others. In April and May these birds form flocks of several thousand individuals which nest in woods, parks, orchards, farmlands (in Scotland and northern England), on the moors, wooded hill slopes, and mountain forests up to 5,000 feet (1,600 m). It usually nests in quite tall trees. Breeding period, April to June, five to six eggs; incubation period, 13–14 days. Nesting period, about 14 days.

In summer it feeds on worms and snails; in winter primarily on berries. Distribution: Europe, Asia, southern Greenland.

Redwing   Colour photo on page 28
(*Turdus iliacus*) 8¼ inches (21 cm)
Family: Flycatcher (Muscicapidae)

The redwing is Europe's smallest thrush. The upper side is brown, the underside whitish with dark spots. It has a striking creamy white eye stripe and beard stripe. The flanks and underwing are reddish. Call: migrating call a high and drawn-out "seeih"; song: a series of falling, flute-like notes "drii-drii-dri-driiee" with a soft twitter at the end. The redwing is only a transient visitor here between late October or early November and April. During severe weather they often move to Ireland and return when conditions improve. In its Scandinavian and north Asiatic breeding grounds it lives in forests and on the edges of the tundra. In Scandinavia it also breeds in parks and gardens. It nests in low trees and bushes and, occasionally, on the ground; five to six eggs; incubation period, 12–15 days; nesting period, 12–14 days.

Feed on insects, slugs, snails, worms, and berries, particularly on grapes in autumn. Distribution: northern Europe, northern Asia.

Song thrush   Colour photos on pages 28 and 38 (Young)
(*Turdus philomelos*) 9 inches (23 cm)
Family: Flycatcher (Muscicapidae)

The breast of the song thrush is buff with dark streaks; the upper side is pale brown, the underside whitish. Sexes alike. Call: mating call a high-pitched "seep"; alarm note "dick-dick-dick". Its song is a series of short, highly contrasting strophes, each of which it repeats two or three times. It also interlaces its own song with those of other birds. The song thrush commonly breeds and feeds in woodlands, parks, orchards, and gardens which have a plentiful supply of trees. It sings from high in the tree, usually at the top. It finds most of its food on the ground. The nest is made from grass and foliage and lined with mud or decayed wood and is usually found low on conifer trees or, more rarely, in bushes. Breeding period from April to July (breeding twice a year), three to six eggs; incubation period, 13 days; nesting period, 14 days.

Feeds on insects and earthworms in summer; in autumn and winter on berries and fruit, too. It will also eat small seeds. Very fond of snails and smashes the shell against a stone. In autumn the song thrush migrates southwards. Only those which breed in Southern and Western Europe stay where they are. Wintering in Central or Northern Europe is an exception. They return early, however, about the beginning of March, and visit feeding places if winter conditions set in again. Distribution: Europe, Asia. A darker variety lives on the islands of the Outer Hebrides and Skye.

Great tit   Colour photos on front and back fly, pages 9 (Young) and 27
(*Parus major*) 5½ inches (14 cm)
Family: Tit (Paridae)

The great tit is the largest of our tits and has a black head with white cheeks, a green-yellow back, and a yellow stomach with a black bib. Sexes alike. Calls are varied (Studies have distinguished approximately 40 different calls from a single bird), but it does have a characteristic "tsee-tsee-deh" or "tea-cher tea-cher", as well as "pink" and "tsidooid". Alarm note, a jarring "cher-r-r". To be seen practically anywhere where there are trees, including in towns. Not at all shy, it is fond of performing acrobatics in trees and bushes and hopping along the ground. The great tit breeds in holes and prefers tree holes and nesting boxes for its nest, but if there is a shortage of these it will take to postboxes, pipes, holes in the wall, and such like. The soft nest is usually made of moss and lined with feathers. Breeding period, April to July, 8–12 eggs; incubation period, 13 days. Nesting period, 15–20 days.

The great tit, like all tits, searches for food whilst hanging from branches with its head down. It will eat insects, especially caterpillars, spiders, seeds, nuts, berries, and buds. It uses its very strong beak to hammer open tough shells, holding the nut with its claws. In winter it is a regular and frequent visitor to feeding places. It has no trouble getting at food left hanging. It holds itself fast with its claws and picks at it. It will take away sun-

Winter Visitors and Breeding Birds

flower seeds one at a time and skilfully break them open. Distribution: Europe, Asia, northwest Africa.

Blue tit   Colour photos on pages 9 and 38
(*Parus caeruleus*) 4½ inches (11.5 cm)
Family: Tit (Paridae)
Noticeably smaller than the great tit, with a light blue upper side, especially the head and tail, white cheeks and forehead; underside yellow with black vertical flecking. Sexes alike. Call: soft "tsee-tsee-tsee", "tsee-tsee-tseer"; excited "tseretete", "tse-tsee-driu", or "tse-tsee-driu-driu". This attractive tit lives in gardens and parks but avoids towns more so than the great tit. It prefers oak forests or other deciduous forests but avoids conifer-only forests. When hunting for food it performs the typical acrobatics of the tit family among the branches, with its head held down. The blue tit, too, breeds in holes. It builds its nest of soft vegetation, feathers, wool, and fibres. [When making artificial holes care should be taken that the entrance has a radius of about 1 inch (27 mm) to prevent bigger and stronger competitors from occupying it.] Breeding period, April to June, 7–14 eggs; incubation period, 14 days. Nesting period, 16–18 days.

In summer it feeds mainly on small insects and their eggs and larvae; in winter it feeds on seeds. Along with great tits the blue tit is the most common visitor to feeding places. It will eat seeds, oat flakes, and suet. Distribution: Europe, Near East, northwest Africa.

Crested tit

(*Parus cristatus*) 4½ inches (11.5 cm)
Family: Tit (Paridae)
The crested tit is immediately recognisable by its crest and its whitish cheeks with the triangular markings. Otherwise it is grey-brown in colour. Sexes alike. Call: a purring "iurrr-r" or even "tsee-tsee-giurr". Has a greater preference for coniferous forests than even the coal tit, especially pine forests. It searches for food very high up in trees. In mountainous terrain it breeds at altitudes of up to 6,000 feet (1900 m). The nest is built in tree holes, stumps, squirrel holes, nesting boxes, or the nests of predatory birds. It is less likely than other tits to accept nesting boxes. Breeding period, April to June (sometimes breeding twice a year), five to eight eggs; incubation period, 13–15 days. Nesting period, 17–21 days.

Feeds mainly on insects but also pine seeds in winter. Appears at feeding places in its usual habitat. Distribution: Europe; *Parus cristatus scoticus* in Scotland; unknown in England.

Marsh tit

(*Parus pallustris*) 4½ inches (11.5 cm)
Family: Tit (Paridae)
The marsh tit is a rather unstriking member of the tit family with its pale grey-brown plumage, silky black crown, and black patch on its throat. Sexes alike. Call: "peez-je-dededed". Song: "deeb-deeb-deeb" or "tsee-tsee-tsee". The marsh tit is found in both deciduous and coniferous forests, in parks, orchards, and gardens, where it can be found performing acrobatics among the branches—often with its stomach uppermost! The mossy nest is built in tree holes; it takes well to nest boxes. Breeding period April to May, seven to eight eggs; incubation period, 12–13 days. Nesting period, 17–20 days.

Feeds mainly on insects in summer; also on seeds in autumn and winter. Will readily make use of feeding places on the edges of towns and villages. Distribution: Europe.

Winter Visitors and Breeding Birds

Coal tit   Colour photo front cover
(*Parus ater*) 4¼ inches (11 cm)
Family: Tit (Paridae)

The smallest Central European tit has similar markings to the great tit but is without any yellow in its plumage and has no black bib on its stomach. Sexes alike. Call: high-pitched and thin "tsee" or "sissee-sissee". Song: "sidiuu-sidiuu" or "witse-witse-witse". The coal tit prefers coniferous forests nesting up to the tree line. It can also be found in mixed forests with isolated groups of conifers as well as in gardens with some cedars, yews, or cypresses. The nest is made in tree holes and stumps; it takes well to nest boxes. Breeding period, April to June (breeding twice a year), 8–10 eggs; incubation period, 14–16 days. Nesting period, 16–17 days.

As with the other tits it feeds mainly on insects in the summer and seeds in the winter; it is also a ready user of feeding places. Distribution: Europe, Asia, northwest Africa.

Nuthatch   Colour photo page 28
(*Sitta europaea*) 5½ inches (14 cm)
Family: Nuthatch (Sittidae)

The nuthatch is a striking bird with blue-grey upper side, buff underside, relatively short tail, long, woodpecker-like beak, and dark eye stripes. Sexes alike. Call: loud and varied, calls "chwit-chwit-chwit", "chweet", or "chewee-chewee-chewee"; song: loud strophes of "vee-vee-vee" or "chewer". Nuthatches live in mixed forests, parks (even in central London), and boulevards: indeed anywhere there are old and tall trees. Its behaviour is very conspicuous. It climbs the trunks, going up and down and across—always with the head to the fore, unlike the woodpecker, which keeps its head up. Nuthatches breed in holes and take readily to holes abandoned by woodpeckers but will also use nest boxes. If the entrance is too large, then the nuthatch will block it up with mud and damp soil so that there is just enough space for it to get through. Builds its nest of bark flakes and leaves. Breeding period, April to June, six to eight eggs; incubation period, 13–15 days. Nesting period, 22–25 days.

Feeds mainly on insects and their larvae; in winter it will also eat various seeds. It uses its strong beak to pull out insects from the bark and channels in the wood and also uses it to crack open nuts, beechnuts, and all varieties of seeds. To open the seeds the bird wedges them in cracks in the wood and then breaks them open with its beak. The nuthatch also stores food in the cracks in the bark. The nuthatch is a frequent visitor to feeding places and livens up the birds' winter scene with its lively antics. Distribution: Europe, Asia, northwest Africa. The bird does not breed in Ireland and is only occasionally recorded in northern England and Scotland.

The yellowhammer feeds on grass seeds and grains in winter. They pick out the oat scraps from horse manure.

62

Winter Visitors and Breeding Birds

Treecreeper

(*Certhia familiaris*) 5 inches (12.5 cm)

Family: Treecreeper (Certhiidae)

The treecreeper is a tobacco-brown bird with a long bobtail and a long downwards-curling beak. The underside is gleaming white with brown flanks, the upper side brown with whitish sides. Sexes alike. Call: ''tee-tee-tee'', extremely high-pitched and loud. Its song is a series of high, thin, long notes. It lives in deciduous and mixed forests as well as gardens and parks. Treecreepers search for their food—insects and their larvae—in the cracks in the bark or in old garden walls with their thin, scythe-like curling beaks. It spirals its way up tree trunks in jerky movements. Once it reaches the top it moves down to the next tree and starts again. On cold nights they sleep in groups and snuggle up close to each other, their heads turned inwards and their tails out. The treecreeper winters in its breeding quarters. It makes its nest under roofs, in cracks in trees, or behind loose or soft bark. They readily use nest boxes made specifically for them. Breeding period, April to August, five to seven eggs; incubation period, 14–15 days. Nesting period, 16–17 days.

Feeds mainly on insects and spiders. Does not usually use feeding places. Distribution: Europe and northwest Africa.

Wren

(*Troglodytes troglodytes*) 3¾ inches (9.5 cm)

Family: Wren (Troglodytidae)

A small bird, scarcely the size of a mouse, with a round dark-brown body, short cocked-up tail, and finely barred upper side and flanks. The underside is light brown. Sexes alike. Call: clear, shrill ''tic-tic-tic''; alarm note ''tserrrr''. Its song is a loud twit-ter and trill with single clear notes. The wren is equally lively in both summer and winter. It is constantly scurrying about, slipping in and out of dense shrubbery, keeping close to the ground, moving along overgrown bushes on riverbanks; it will suddenly spring onto a raised vantage point and sing its astonishingly clear song. To be found in parks, gardens, and forest, wherever there is sufficient dense undergrowth. (A recent survey showed that this tiny, brown bird was the most common nesting bird in England and Ireland, with a total population of approximately 10 million.) The dome-shaped nest, with its entrance at the side, is well hidden in the undergrowth or among the creepers on a house wall or in the tangled roots of fallen trees. The male prepares several nests in spring, and the female chooses one of them. Breeding period, April to July (breeding twice a year), five to seven eggs; incubation period, 14–16 days. Nesting period, 15–18 days.

As a resident bird the wren continues during the winter to hunt for spiders and insects and their eggs and larvae. Wrens only rarely visit feeding places. Distribution: Europe, Asia, northwest Africa, North America.

Yellowhammer

(*Emberiza citrinella*) 6½ inches (16.5 cm)

Family: Bunting (Emberizidae)

The head is a golden yellow; the crown and cheeks are edged in brown. The back and wings are a yellowish brown colour; the rump is a cinnamon brown, and the blackish tail has white edges; the underside is yellow, and the flanks and breast have brownish streaks. The female is less striking, being more brown and with more streaks. Call: ''tsreek'', ''tsiurr'', or ''tseep-tsee-tsee''; its song a monotone strophe ''tsee-tsee-tsee-

tsee–beeeh''. The yellowhammer is not only the most strikingly coloured but also the most common of our buntings. Their numbers, however, are in decline. It lives on the edges of the forest, copses, hedgerows, and pine nurseries. The male sings from high perching places, such as branches, telegraph wires, or poles. The nest is built by the female on the ground or in low, dense scrub and is kept well hidden. Breeding period, April to July (mostly breeding twice a year), three to five eggs; incubation period, 12–13 days. Nesting period, 9–14 days.

Feeds on insects and fine seeds; feeding primarily on seeds in autumn and winter. Yellowhammers form swarms in the autumn and hunt for food together in the fields and villages. They readily visit feeding places but look for their food mainly on the ground. Distribution: Europe, Asia.

Brambling   Colour photos pages 27 and 55
(*Fringilla montifringilla*)   6 inches (15 cm)
Family: Finch (Fringillidae)

The head and tail feathers of the male, which are black during the breeding season, are edged in light brown in winter, making the brambling less noticeable. On the whole the females look browner. Call: a squeaking ''kvaik-kvaik'' or ''shrooee''; when taking flight ''yekk-yekk''. Bramblings are only winter visitors here (October to March) or transitory migrants. They breed in the Far North, mainly in birch forests but also in mixed and coniferous forests. Breeding period, May to July, five to seven eggs; incubation period, 13 days. Nesting period, 12–14 days.

Bramblings search for beechnuts as their main source of food in their winter quarters, but they also come to feeding places—often in great numbers—where they spend most of their time on the ground. Distribution: Northern Europe and northern Asia.

Chaffinch   Colour photos pages 38 (young bird) and 55
(*Fringilla coelebs*) 6 inches (15 cm)
Family: Finch (Fringillidae)

The breeding plumage of the male is blue-grey at the sides and back of the neck, the crown, and around the beak and chestnut at the sides of the head and underside. The dark wings have two striking white bars. The males appear less colourful in winter. Females and young have olive-brown upper sides and pale grey-brown undersides. Call: mating call ''pink'' or a soft ''fooeed'', also ''triuiud'' and ''rreet''. The song of the finch is a fixed strophe ''tseetseetseetsye-tsyetsyatsyatsya-tsorkeek-chuchick''. The chaffinch is one of our most common woodland birds. Only in the cities is it outnumbered by the blackbird. Chaffinches live in gardens, parks, coppices, open landscapes with hedges and clumps of trees, and in coniferous forests, too. The female builds its soft nest in a deep cup shape of moss, lichen, and stalks. Breeding period, April to June, three to six eggs; incubation period, 13 days. Nesting period, 13–14 days.

Chaffinches feed themselves and their young on insects. In autumn and winter they feed on seeds and greenery. The chaffinches from the northeastern breeding grounds migrate to Central and Southern Europe in autumn, the females going farther than the males. Those that stay in winter form large swarms with other finches and buntings. At feeding places they eat seeds, oats, and bread crumbs. Distribution: Europe, western Asia, northwest Africa.

Winter Visitors and Breeding Birds

Greenfinch   Colour photo page 55
(*Chloris chloris*) 5¾ inches (14.5 cm)
Family: Finch (Carduelidae)

The greenfinch has a very strong beak. In the males the outer wing feathers and the outer tail feathers have striking yellow markings; the remaining plumage is an olive green. The females appear a more grey-green, as do the young. Call: mating call "jooee"; on takeoff, "giu-giu-giu". The song of the male is a canary-like trill mixed with whistling notes and imitations of other bird songs. Greenfinches live in towns and villages—in parks, churchyards, and orchards—and in mixed open forests. The female builds its nest of moss, grasses, roots, and plant fibres in dense hedges, bushes, or trees. Breeding period, April to August, four to six eggs; incubation period, 13 days. Nesting period, 13–16 days.

The nestlings are fed on a pulpy vegetable food from their parents' crops. Even the older birds feed on buds, seeds, and berries. In winter greenfinches are one of the most frequent visitors to feeding places where, however, they behave quite quarrelsomely, forcefully maintaining their place against weaker birds. They are particularly fond of sunflower seeds, hemp seeds, and other seeds. Distribution: Europe, western Asia, northwest Africa.

Siskin   Colour photo page 10
(*Carduelis spinus*) 4¾ inches (12 cm)
Family: Finch (Carduelidae)

The siskin is a graceful, yellow-green finch with a black crown, small black chin, and a pointed awl-shaped beak. Call: in flight a hoarse "dee-eh"; contact call "det-dettdet". Song—often performed in flight—"deedee-dee-deee-deediedeh". The siskin lives in mountain forests up to 6,000 feet (1,800 m), in small breeding populations in the pine woods of the Highlands, conifer and mixed forests, and larger parks. They can be seen in flocks in winter, tumbling about in birch trees and alders searching for seeds. Occasionally the whole flock will fly off, only to return to the same or a neighbouring tree almost immediately. The nest is made of fine twigs, stalks, moss, and lichen and is usually located higher than 15 feet (5 m) up a pine tree on an outside branch. Breeding period, April to July (breeding twice a year), four to six eggs; incubation period, 13 days. Nesting period, 13–15 days.

Feeds on insects and aphids in the summer and seeds in winter. Distribution: Europe, Asia.

Bullfinch
(*Pyrrhula pyrrhula*) 5¾–6¾ inches (14.5–16 cm)
Family: Finch (Carduelidae)

The male has a black head, black wings, and a black tail. The back is silver-grey and the stomach wine-red. The female and young have less red and are generally drabber. A white bar on the wings is a striking feature of both sexes. Call: mating call a soft "deuu"; contact call "beet-beet". The song of the male is a gentle chattering sound with a mixture of squeaking and piping tones. Bullfinches live in conifer and mixed forests, parks, and gardens. The females build the nest in dense hedges or conifers. Breeding period, April to July, four to seven eggs; incubation period, 13 days. Nesting period, 16 days.

Adult birds feed mainly on a vegetarian fare, such as buds, shoots, and seeds, and mainly on berries in autumn. The young also eat insects as part of their diet. The bullfinches here winter in their breeding quarters, and their numbers are swelled by others which breed farther north. They readily visit feeding places, where they eat seeds and berries. Distribution: Europe, Asia—separate species.

Crossbill   Colour photo on page 55
(*Loxia curvirostra*) 6½ inches (16.5 cm)
Family: Finch (Carduelidae)

The males have a reddish orange plumage and the females a yellowish green. Wings and tail are black-brown. The tips of the bill are crossed. Call: in flight a clear "jip-jip". Its song is made up of repetitions of various two- or three-syllabled piping notes. Crossbills are one of the "gypsy" breed of birds that move over wide distances (especially in Scotland and east of London) and settle and breed wherever they can find a good source of food. They are very gregarious. When looking for food they move about acrobatically, climbing and hanging in conifers. The nest is positioned high up in conifers. Breeding period: at any season, though principally in the last months of winter, three to four eggs; incubation period, 12–14 days. Nesting period, about 14 days.

Feeds on seeds from pine trees and other conifers. Distribution: Europe, Asia, northwest Africa, North America.

Parrot crossbill
(*Loxia pytyopsittacus*) 6¾ inches (17 cm)
Family: Finch (Carduelidae)

A very similar bird to the crossbill. It is, however, somewhat larger and has a stronger bill. Call: similar to the crossbill but with a deeper "koepp-koepp" and "giup-giup". Song same as the crossbill. Behaviour is similar, too. The parrot crossbill is mainly to be found in pine forests. The breeding quarters are mainly in northern Europe. Breeds throughout the year, depending on the availability of food, though mainly in the final winter months; three to five eggs; incubation period, 14–16 days. Nesting period, about 14 days.

Pine seeds are its main food. Distribution: northern Europe.

Hawfinch   Colour photo page 55
(*Coccothraustes coccothraustes*) 7 inches (18 cm)
Family: Finch (Carduelidae)

The hawfinch—the largest native finch—has an outsize-looking bill. The male is light coloured, with darker pastel-brown colouring, and orange-brown head; the bill is blue-grey. The female is paler. Call: a sharp "tsick", "tsititt". Its song is a rarely heard, quiet twittering. Favoured nesting places are mixed and deciduous forests with oak and beech groves, coppices, and larger parks. The hawfinch is rarely seen, as it perches high up in the trees. The female builds the relatively large nest of twigs, roots, and stalks, mainly in deciduous trees or bushes. Breeding period, May to June (breeding once a year), four to six eggs; incubation period, 12–14 days. Nesting period, 11–14 days.

The adult birds feed mainly on the seeds of deciduous trees and stone fruit—though they do not eat the flesh of the fruit. Their bills are so strong that they can even break open the stones of cherries and plums. The young are also fed insects. The hawfinch is a frequent visitor to feeding places in winter. Distribution: Europe, Asia, northwest Africa.

House sparrow   Colour photo of young on page 38
(*Passer domesticus*) 5¾ inches (15 cm)
Family: Sparrow (Passeridae)

Winter Visitors and Breeding Birds

During the breeding season the top of the male's head is grey with a chestnut neck, a black throat bib, and whitish cheeks. The upper side is chestnut with black speckles; the underside is light grey. The female is less distinguished and without the black bib. Call: the loud chirping and cheeping are well known; the male has a chatty and chirpy song. It is well known that the house sparrow lives exclusively amongst people. A clean house sparrow, free of dust and soot, is a very pretty sight. However, both adult and young birds are very fond of rolling in loose sand and earth. House sparrows always appear in groups, often breeding in colonies. In the search for a mate there are often fights amongst the males. During mating the male hops about the female with its wings hanging down and its tail up. Any hole or cavity will do for a nest. The large nest, which is usually domed, is made of grass and feathers and built under tiles, in wall cavities and chimneys, and in abandoned swallows' nests and nest boxes. If storks are nesting nearby, house sparrows will move in as "lodgers". Breeding period, April to August, four to six eggs; incubation period, 11–14 days. Nesting period, 13–14 days.

Feeds on seeds, berries, fruit, buds, insects, and all manner of human waste. In winter they depend on cereal and other waste products and plunder feeding places with relish. Distribution: Wherever there are people.

Tree sparrow
(*Passer montanus*) 5½ inches (14 cm)
Family: Sparrow (Passeridae)

The male and female, which are somewhat smaller and more delicate than the house sparrow, are alike; the top of the head is chestnut brown, the cheeks white with a black spot on each cheek, and the throat, light brown with dark marking and a light underside. Call: "chick-chick-chok" and a clamouring "teck-teck". Its song consists of chirping noises. In summer, tree sparrows live outside towns and villages in open woodlands and parks where trees with tree holes offer an opportunity for breeding. In winter they move closer to settlements or their outskirts. They do not, however, move into town. The domed nest, made of blades of grass, straw, and feathers, is built in tree holes, nest boxes, and, more rarely, in wall cavities. Breeding period, April to August (breeding up to three times a year), four to six eggs; incubation period, 13–14 days. Nesting period, 14–16 days.

Like the house sparrow, the tree sparrow feeds on seeds, berries, fruit, buds, and insects. In winter, they come to feeding places and feed on grain and other seeds, oat flakes, and bread crumbs. Distribution: Europe and Asia, introduced into North America and Australia by human migrants.

Starling
Colour photo page 10
(*Sturnus vulgaris*) 8½ inches (21.5 cm)
Family: Starling (Sturnidae)

The plumage is an iridescent black, green, and violet with light-grey speckles. The bill is yellow and the tail relatively short. In winter the feather tips are lighter, which makes it appear more spotted. The young are grey-brown and unspotted. Sexes alike. Call: alarm note a harsh "spett spett", "reh", or a hissing "bohrr". Its song consists of chattering, grating, clicking, and purring notes, mixed with imitations of other bird songs. Starlings are skilled mimics and weave all manner of sounds into their song. Starlings are amongst the best known native birds as they live in close proximity to human beings and so gather in large flocks, especially in spring and autumn. Starlings live in deciduous and mixed forests, parks, and gardens. In autumn and spring they form enormous flocks and rest for the night in reeds, groups of trees, or overgrown buildings. They breed in tree holes, under roof tiles, in wall cavities, and in nest boxes [the entrance hole in a nest box for starlings must have a radius of 1¾ inches (45 mm).] The nest is very untidily built of blades of grass, straw, and feathers. Breeding period, April to July, four to six eggs; incubation period, 12–14 days. Nesting period, 18–22 days.

During the breeding period starlings mainly feed on an animal diet on which they also feed the nestlings. They look for food on the ground and move aside the earth in a circling motion with their open bills. When they "invade" vineyards and orchards in large swarms in summer and autumn they can cause considerable damage. Starlings are partial migrants. Some of those that breed in northeast Europe winter in Central Europe; those that breed in Central Europe migrate to Southern and Western Europe. The return begins very early in spring so that starlings are amongst the first birds to reappear with the onset of mild weather, often as early as February. They mostly appear at feeding places if there is continued snow or a resurgence of winter weather in spring. They are fond of oat flakes, suet, and small seeds. Distribution: Europe and western Asia. Introduced into North America and Australia by humans.

Jay
(*Garrulus glandarius*) 13½ inches (34 cm)
Family: Crow (Corvidae)
The jay is the most colourful of our crows.

The body plumage is bright russet with a black beard stripe going from the bill to beneath the eyes; feathers are black and white with striking blue-and-black striped primaries. The head feathers can be erected to form a crest. Call: a harsh scolding screech, especially when used as an alarm note. Its song can only be heard at close quarters, a quiet chatter with more or less melodic inserts mixed with imitations of other bird songs. Jays live in all forests and stray into parks in cities and pass through villages. The nest is built in trees and bushes. Breeding period, April to June, five to six eggs; incubation period, 16–17 days. Nesting period, 19–20 days. The fledglings are similar in colour to the parents.

Feed on insects but also on eggs and young of small birds whose nests the jays skilfully detect. In autumn they often band together. They then search for winter supplies, especially acorns, which they hide on the ground. They are not infrequent visitors to feeding places, where they eat suet, larger seeds, and grain, as well as pieces of meat and berries. Distribution: Europe, Asia, northwest Africa.

Magpie
(*Pica pica*) 18 inches (46 cm)
Family: Crow (Corvidae)
The magpie is quite a striking bird with its black-and-white plumage and a long graduated tail which accounts for almost half of its length. The young have a shorter tail and matt plumage. Sexes alike. Call: a raw "shackackack" or a clear "yeckyeck". Its song is a subdued, jay-like chatter with grating sounds. Magpies live in open landscapes with trees and bushes, in parks, and—increasingly in recent times—in towns and villages. They have even been reported in the

Winter Visitors and Breeding Birds

parks and gardens of our largest cities. The nest is sometimes situated in quite low hedges and bushes, as well as in high trees. The nest is a domed construction of twigs, often lined with mud. Breeding period, March to April, five to eight eggs; incubation period, 17–18 days. Nesting period, 22–24 days.

Magpies feed on insects, small vertebrates, and birds' eggs, but berries and fruit also form part of their diet. Magpies rarely visit feeding places, and when they do they behave in a very shy manner. Distribution: Europe, Asia, northwest Africa, North America.

Further Reading

Brunn, B., and Singer, A. *The Hamlyn Guide to Birds of Britain and Europe*. Hamlyn, London, 1970.

Fisher, J., and Flegg, J. J. M. *Watching Birds*. Poyser, Berkhampstead, 1974.

Fitter, R., et al. *Book of British Birds*. Reader's Digest/AA, Collins, 1969.

Gooders, J. *How to Watch Birds*. Andre Deutsch, London, 1975.

Hayman, P., and Burton, P. *The Birdlife of Britain*. Mitchell Beazley, London, 1976.

Hollom, P. A. D. *The Popular Handbook of British Birds*. Witherby, London, 1968.

Lack, D. *Life of the Robin*. Witherby, London, 1977.

Murton, R. *Man and Birds*. Collins, London, 1977.

Newton, I. *Finches*. Collins, London, 1972.

Perrins, C. *Birds*. Collins, London, 1974.

Peterson, R. T., Mountfort, G., and Hollom, P. A. D. *A Field Guide to the Birds of Britain and Europe*. Collins, London, 1966.

Saunders, D. *RSPB Guide to British Birds*. Hamlyn, London, 1975.

Sharrock, T. T. R. *The Atlas of Breeding Birds in Britain and Ireland*. Irish Wildlife Conservancy/British Trust for Ornithology, Tring, 1976.

Soper, T. *Everyday Birds*. David and Charles, Newton Abbot, 1976.

Sparks, J. *Bird Behaviour*. Hamlyn, London, 1969.

Sparks, J., and Soper, T. *Owls: Their Natural and Unnatural History*. David and Charles, Newton Abbot, 1970.

Books that deal with different aspects of
    birds and wildlife in the garden:
Barrington, R. *The Bird Gardener's Book*.
    Wolfe, London, 1971.
Burton, R. *Ponds, Their Wildlife and Up-
    keep*. David and Charles, Newton Abbot,
    1977.
Chinery, M. *The Natural History of the Gar-
    den*. Collins, London, 1977.
Flegg, J. J. M., and Glue, D. E. *Nestboxes*.
    British Trust for Ornithology, Tring,
    1971.
Soper, T. *The Bird Table Book in Colour*.
    David and Charles, Newton Abbot, 1977.

Bird Conservation Societies

The Royal Society for the Protection of Birds,
The Lodge,
Sandy,
Bedfordshire.

The Young Ornithologists' Club,
The Lodge,
Sandy,
Bedfordshire.

The British Trust for Ornithology,
Beech Grove,
Tring,
Hertfordshire.

The Society for the Promotion of
    Nature Conservation
The Green,
Nettleham,
Lincolnshire.

Index

Index